Get the eBook FREE!

(PDF, ePub, Kindle, and liveBook all included)

We believe that once you buy a book from us, you should be able to read it in any format we have available. To get electronic versions of this book at no additional cost to you, purchase and then register this book at the Manning website.

Go to https://www.manning.com/freebook and follow the instructions to complete your pBook registration.

That's it!
Thanks from Manning!

How Computers Make Books

How Computers Make Books

JOHN WHITINGTON

MANNING

SHELTER ISLAND

Manning Publications Co.	Development editor: Doug Rudder
20 Baldwin Road	Technical editor: Bojan Stojanović
PO Box 761	Review editor: Aleksandar Dragosavljević
Shelter Island, NY 11964	Production editor: Keri Hales
	Copy editor: Alisa Larson
	Proofreader: Jason Everett
	Typesetter: Westchester Publishing Services
	Cover designer: Marija Tudor

ISBN: 9781633438675
Printed in the United States of America

brief contents

contents

preface

It can be tremendously difficult for an outsider to understand why computer scientists are interested in computer science. It is easy to see the sense of wonder of the astrophysicist or the evolutionary biologist or zoologist. We don't know too much about the mathematician, but we are in awe anyway. But computer science? Well, we suppose it must have to do with computers at least. "Computer science is no more about computers than astronomy is about telescopes," wrote the great Dutch computer scientist Edsger Dijkstra (1930–2002). That is to say, the computer is our tool for exploring this subject and for building things in its world, but it is not the world itself.

This book makes no attempt at completeness whatsoever. It is a set of little sketches of the use of computer science to address the problems of book production. By looking from different angles at interesting challenges and pretty solutions, we hope to gain some insight into the essence of the thing.

I hope that, by the end, you will have some understanding of why these topics interest computer scientists, and perhaps you will find that some of them interest you.

acknowledgments

This book has its origins in knowledge created, found and gathered elsewhere—methods and mechanisms honed over decades or centuries. It could not have been written without the inventions it describes, as you will see.

At Manning, Ian Hough and Andy Waldron in Acquisitions took a chance on this rather unusual book, helping to shape its contents and structure. My patient development editor, Doug Rudder, shepherded the book through development and writing. Bojan Stovanović, my technical editor, and Benjamin Berg, LaTeX expert, came to the rescue with my frequent typesetting problems. The production team polished the book into what you're reading today.

Finally, I'd like to thank the reviewers: Charles Mike Shelton, Christopher Villanueva, Darrin Bishop, Eddy Vluggen, Enric Garcia Torrents, Fatih Ozer, Giampiero Granatella, Howard Bandy, James J. Byleckie, Jaume Lopez, Jeff Neumann, Jens Christian B. Madsen, Jeremy Bryan, Jose Alberto Reyes Quevedo, Kathleen R. Estrada, Lewis Van Winkle, Manu Sareena, Manuel Ciosici, Roberto Hirata Jr., Romain Jouin, Tim Wooldridge, To Tuan Nghia, Tony Dubitsky, and Ubaldo Pescatore, as well as the Manning Early Access Program customers for their time and invaluable comments on earlier drafts of the manuscript. Their suggestions helped make this a better book.

about this book

How do we decide where to put ink on a page to draw letters and pictures? How can computers represent all the world's languages and writing systems? What exactly is a computer program, what and how does it calculate, and how can we build one? Can we compress information to make it easier to store and quicker to transmit? How do newspapers print photographs with gray tones using just black ink and white paper? How are paragraphs laid out automatically on a page and split across multiple pages?

We answer these questions and more, taking a meandering tour of the art and science of book production from ancient times to the modern day, looking at both the low-level technical details and the overall landscape. You won't need any prior knowledge of publishing or computer programming to enjoy this book—just a quiet place and a curious mind.

How this book is organized: A road map

Chapter 1 introduces the book and explains who it is for and why it was written. We then start our exploration from nothing. We have a plain white page on which to place marks in ink to make letters and pictures. How do we decide where to put the ink? How can we draw a convincing straight line? Using a microscope, we will look at the effect of putting these marks on real paper using different printing techniques.

Chapter 2 shows how to draw letters from a realistic typeface—letters that are made from curves and not just straight lines. We will see how typeface designers create such beautiful shapes and how we might draw them on the page. A little geometry is involved, but nothing that can't be done with a pen and paper and a ruler. We fill these shapes to draw letters on the page and deal with some surprising complications.

Chapter 3 describes how computers and communication equipment deal with human language, rather than just the numbers, which are their native tongue. We see how the world's languages may be encoded in a standard form and how we can tell the computer to display our text in different ways.

Chapter 4 introduces some actual computer programming in the context of a method for conducting a search through an existing text to find pertinent words, as we might when constructing an index. We write a real program to search for a word in a given text and look at ways to measure and improve its performance. We see how search engines use these techniques every day.

Chapter 5 explores how to get a book's worth of information into a computer. After a historical interlude concerning typewriters and similar devices from the 19th and early 20th centuries, we consider modern methods. Then we look at how the Asian languages can be typed, even those with hundreds of thousands or millions of symbols.

Chapter 6 deals with compression—that is, making words and images take up less space without losing essential detail. However fast and capacious computers have become, it is still necessary to keep things as small as possible. As a practical example, we consider the method of compression used when sending faxes.

Chapter 7 introduces more programming but of a slightly different kind. We begin by seeing how computer programs calculate simple sums, following the familiar rules we learn in school. We then build more complicated things involving the processing of lists of items. By the end of the chapter, we will have written a substantive, real program.

Chapter 8 addresses the problem of reproducing color or grayscale images using just black ink on white paper. How can we do this convincingly and automatically? We look at historical solutions to this problem from medieval times onward and try out some different modern methods for ourselves, comparing the results.

Chapter 9 looks again at typefaces. We investigate the typeface Palatino and some of its intricacies. We begin to see how letters are laid out next to each other to form a line of words on the page.

Chapter 10 shows how to format a full book page by describing how lines of letters are combined into paragraphs to build up a block of text. We learn how to split words with hyphens at the end of lines without ugliness, and we look at how this sort of formatting was done before computers.

Chapter 11 finishes up, showing how our book gets into the hands of the reader, either in print or electronically. Along the way, we learn the details of the PDF standard for document exchange, which combines text, fonts, drawings, and photographs into a single unit.

liveBook discussion forum

Purchase of *How Computers Make Books* includes free access to liveBook, Manning's online reading platform. Using liveBook's exclusive discussion features, you can attach comments to the book globally or to specific sections or paragraphs. It's a snap to make notes for yourself, ask and answer technical questions, and receive help from the author

and other users. To access the forum, go to https://livebook.manning.com/book/how
-computers-make-books/discussion. You can also learn more about Manning's forums
and the rules of conduct at https://livebook.manning.com/discussion.

Manning's commitment to our readers is to provide a venue where a meaningful
dialogue between individual readers and between readers and the author can take place.
It is not a commitment to any specific amount of participation on the part of the author,
whose contribution to the forum remains voluntary (and unpaid). We suggest you try
asking the author some challenging questions lest his interest stray! The forum and the
archives of previous discussions will be accessible from the publisher's website as long
as the book is in print.

about the author

JOHN WHITINGTON founded a company that builds software for electronic document processing. He studied and taught computer science at Queens' College, Cambridge. He has written textbooks before, but this is his first book for a popular audience.

about the cover

The figure on the cover of *How Computers Make Books* is "Marchande de Miel à Vienne," or "Honey Merchant of Vienna," taken from a collection by Jacques Grasset de Saint-Sauveur, published in 1788. Each illustration is finely drawn and colored by hand.

In those days, it was easy to identify where people lived and what their trade or station in life was just by their dress. Manning celebrates the inventiveness and initiative of the computer business with book covers based on the rich diversity of regional culture centuries ago, brought back to life by pictures from collections such as this one.

Putting marks on paper

This chapter covers

- What this book is about, who it is for, and what it contains
- Coordinates and units for placing ink on a page or pixels on a screen
- The physical characteristics of paper, ink, and computer screens
- Building lines and making shapes using only dots

This book provides an introduction to computer science through a series of sketches highlighting aspects of one central theme: book production. If you are reading a physical paperback copy of this book, everything from the writer's thoughts up to the act of printing it was done automatically. If you are reading this book as an eBook, of course, the book is still inside the computer.

What is computer science? Is it just programming? Is it really a science like physics or chemistry, or is it just a branch of mathematics? Or is it just a fancy way of talking about how we use computers and not a science at all? We will try to answer these questions through eleven sketches based on our theme. This is not a comprehensive, beginning-to-end textbook of book publishing but a look at the techniques behind some important aspects involved in the process. It won't teach you a new programming language or technology, but it should give you insight into the ways we use computers to automate human processes, how we marshal data and computing power to do our work for us, and how the publishing industry uses computers to build electronic and physical books.

We'll look at the science and mathematics behind everything from fonts to photographs, from the transmission and storage of data to the layout of a page, and from the low-level 0s and 1s of a computer's most basic arithmetic to the input and processing of the world's languages. Along the way, we will learn about some of the art and science behind typesetting and printing from the early computer era and from the time before computers. If this appeals to you, read on.

In this chapter, we start right from the beginning: a blank page and some means of placing marks on it. This might be black ink on a piece of paper or pixels on a phone, tablet, eBook reader, or computer screen. We will learn how to choose where to place these marks on the page to build lines and filled shapes. Thereby, we will see how even complex text and graphics are composed of just these little marks.

1.1   *Where things go*

In this book, we will need very little formal mathematics, but if we are considering the arrangement of letters and words and lines and pictures on the page, we will need a way of discussing the idea of position—that is to say, *where* something is, rather than just *what* it is. Thankfully, our paper is flat and rectangular so we can use the simple coordinates we learned in school. In other words, we just measure how far we are above the bottom-left corner of the page and how far to the right. We can write this as a pair of numbers—for example, the coordinate (6, 2) is six lengths right and two lengths up from the bottom-left of the page. It is the convention to use x to denote the across part of the coordinate and y to denote the up part. These are known as *Cartesian* coordinates, named for French mathematician and philosopher René Descartes (1596–1659). The Latin form of his name is Renatus Cartesius, which is a little closer to "Cartesian." The idea was discovered independently, at about the same time, by Pierre de Fermat (1607–1665). Figure 1.1 shows the coordinate (6, 2) drawn on a graph with axes for x and y and little marks on the axes to make it easier to judge position by eye.

We can assign units if we like, such as centimeters or inches, to define what these "lengths" are. In publishing, we like to use a little unit called a *point* or *pt*, which is 1/72 of an inch. This unit is convenient because it allows us to talk mostly using whole numbers (it is easier to talk about 450pt than about 6.319 inches). We need such small units because the items on our page are quite small and must be carefully positioned (look at the writing on this page and see how each tiny little shape representing a character is so carefully placed). Figure 1.2 shows how an A4 page (which is about 595pt wide and about 842pt tall) might look.

You can see that the chapter heading "Chapter 1" begins at about (80, 630). Notice that the coordinates of the bottom left of the page (called the *origin*) are, of course, (0, 0). The choice of the bottom left as our origin is somewhat arbitrary—one could

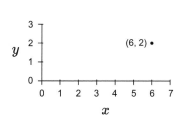

Figure 1.1 Placing a point using Cartesian coordinates

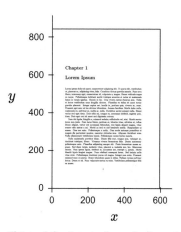

Figure 1.2 A page, its contents, and its units

make an argument that the top-left point, with vertical positions measured downward, is a more appropriate choice, at least in the West where we read top to bottom. Of course, one could also have the origin at the top right or bottom right, with horizontal positions measuring leftward.

We will use such coordinates to describe the position and shape of each part of each letter, each word, and each paragraph, as well as any drawings or photographs to be placed on the page. We will see how lines can be drawn between coordinates and how to make the elegant curves that form the letters in a typeface (sometimes called a *font*).

1.2 Placing dots

Once we have determined what shapes we wish to put on each page, we must consider the final form of our document. You may be reading this as a physical paperback book, printed and bound by very expensive equipment. You may be reading it as an electronic document (such as a PDF) on your computer, tablet, or smartphone. Or, you may be reading it on some sort of special-purpose eBook reader. Each of these scenarios has different characteristics. Every page of the printed book is made up of hundreds of millions of little dots, each of which may be white (no ink) or black (ink). We cannot typically see the dots with the naked eye. The number of dots in a given space is known as the *resolution* (from the word *resolve*). A low-resolution image is one that the eye can easily resolve (that is, distinguish) the individual dots. A high-resolution image has dots so small and tightly packed that the naked eye cannot distinguish them.

A high-resolution printer, such as the one printing the physical copy of this book, may have as many as 600 or 1,200 dots per inch (dpi)—that is, between $600 \times 600 = 360,000$ and $1,200 \times 1,200 = 1,440,000$ dots per square inch. The screen of a computer or tablet may only have 100 to 300 dpi, but it can display many shades of gray and colors. If the resolution is too low, we see blocky images. Figure 1.3 shows part of a capital letter A in black and white at 60 dpi, 30 dpi, and 15 dpi.

Figure 1.3   **Three different resolutions**

We have used square dots here, such as may be used on a modern computer screen (we call them *pixels*, which is short for "picture elements"). For viewing a page on a typical tablet computer, we might have only $2,048 \times 1,536 = 5,193,728$ dots on the whole screen, but they may be colors or grays, as well as black or white. When printing a book like this, we have many more dots, but only in black ink. Let's say, for example, that we have a US Letter page (8.5×11 inches) and we are printing at a resolution of 1,200 dpi. We have $1,200 \times 1,200 = 1,440,000$ dots per square inch, so we have $1,200 \times 1,200 \times 8.5 \times 11$, or 134,640,000 dots on the page, each of which may be black or white.

Figure 1.4 shows photographs, taken under a microscope, of lettering as it appears in high-quality printing and on the much lower-quality, cheaper newsprint used for the daily newspaper.

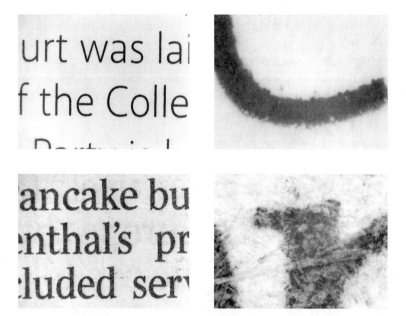

Figure 1.4   **Microscope pictures of high-quality printing (upper) and newsprint (lower)**

The upper row of figure 1.4 shows high-resolution printing of lettering on coated paper, such as might be used for a glossy pamphlet, under a microscope at $20 \times$ magnification and the same at $400 \times$ magnification. The lower row is standard text of the *London Times* printed on newsprint at $20 \times$ magnification and the same at $400 \times$ magnification.

The home or office laser printer works by using a laser to prepare a roller in such a way that a powder will adhere only to areas where the laser has been shone. The powder (called toner) is then transferred from the roller to paper and bonded to it by heat. Figure 1.5 shows that the particles of toner behave rather differently from ink.

Figure 1.5   Microscope pictures of laser-printed text

On the left is a word printed in 1pt, 2pt, 4pt, 6pt, and 8pt text under a microscope, with magnification at 20×. On the right, the 2pt word with magnification at 400× (a typeface of a given size is roughly that number of points tall, say, for its capital letters.)

If we were to store each page of our documents electronically as collections of millions of these dots, it would form a huge amount of information that would be costly and difficult to manipulate and transmit. So, we will normally store our pages in a more structured way—some paragraphs, which are made of words, which are made of letters, which are drawn from some typeface, which is defined using lines and curves. The hundreds of millions of dots that will finally make up the page only exist temporarily as the image is printed or placed onto the screen. (The exception, of course, is when we use photographs as part of our page—the color of each dot is captured by the camera, and we must maintain it in that form.) Until recently, the storage, transmission, and manipulation of high-resolution photographs was a significant problem. The storage, transmission, and manipulation of high-resolution video still is—imagine how many little colored dots make up a still image and then multiply by 25 or 50 images per second for the 2 hours (7,200 seconds) a feature film lasts.

1.3   *Making lines*

We have talked only about single dots. However, we will need lines, curves, and filled shapes to build our page. Suppose that we wish to draw a line. How can we work out which dots to paint black to represent the line? Horizontal and vertical lines seem easy—we just put ink on each dot in that row or column for the whole length of the line. If we want a thicker line, we can ink multiple rows or columns on either side of the original line. But there are many useful lines other than horizontal and vertical ones. To begin, we will need a way to define a line. We can use two coordinates—those of the points at either end. For example, figure 1.6 shows the line (1, 1)—(6, 3).

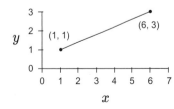

Figure 1.6   A line defined by the coordinates of its two endpoints

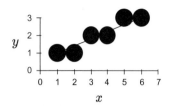

Figure 1.7 Approximating a line with six dots

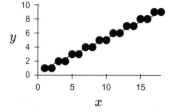

Figure 1.8 Approximating a line with 18 dots

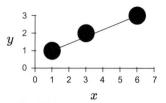

Figure 1.9 The wrong approach: one dot per row

In mathematics, we would usually consider a line to be of infinite length, and so the line in figure 1.6 is really a line *segment*, but we will just call it a line. Notice that this line could equally be defined as $(6, 3)$—$(1, 1)$.

As a first strategy, let's try coloring in one dot in each column from column 1 to column 6, where the line is present. Figure 1.7 shows the result of choosing the dot whose center is closest to the line in each case. Admittedly, figure 1.7 does not look much like a line. But if we choose a higher resolution for a line of the same slope, thus drawing more and smaller dots, we see a better approximation, as shown in figure 1.8.

Now, you may wonder why we chose to draw one dot in each column instead of one dot in each row. For example, instead of putting one dot in each of the columns from column 1 to column 6, we might put one dot in each of the rows from row 1 to row 3, again choosing the one in that row nearest the actual line. For this shallow line, doing so would lead to a most unpleasant result, as shown in figure 1.9.

If the line is steeper than 45°, the converse is true (draw it on paper to see). So, we choose to put one black dot in each row instead of in each column in this case. Horizontal and vertical lines are simply special cases of this general method: for the vertical case, we draw one dot in each row, and for the horizontal case, we draw one dot in each column. For the line at exactly 45°, the two methods (row and column) produce the same result. Figure 1.10 illustrates the sorts of patterns of dots we see for lines of various slopes using this improved procedure.

The image in figure 1.10 is 100 dots tall and wide. The results are not terribly good for two reasons. First, at low resolutions, the individual dots are clearly visible. Second, the density of the lines varies. A horizontal or vertical line of length 100 will have 100 dots over its length, but the 45° line has 100 dots over a length of about 141 (the diagonal of a square with sides of length 100 is $\sqrt{2} \times 100$), so its density of dots is lower, and it appears less dark.

When we are using a screen, rather than paper, to display our line, we can take advantage of the ability to

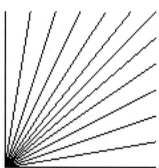

Figure 1.10 Lines of differing slopes

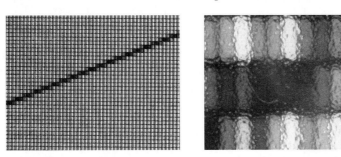

Figure 1.11 Using shades of gray for smoother lines

Figure 1.12 A shape filled first with black and white dots and then with dots of differing shades of gray

use more than just black and white. And so, we can use varying shades of gray: dots right on the line are very dark gray, and dots that are just close are lighter gray. Figure 1.11 shows a line drawn in this manner at three scales.

We can see that the line in figure 1.11 is smoother than would otherwise be the case. If you are reading this book on an electronic device, you may be able to see this effect on the text or images with a magnifying glass. Figure 1.12 shows another example with a more complex, filled shape, which might be used to represent an ampersand character.

The image on the left in figure 1.12 is an idealized high-resolution shape. The image in the middle is just black and white at a lower resolution, and the image on the right is prepared for display on a screen supporting gray as well as black and white at the same lower resolution. This use of grays is known as *anti-aliasing* since the jagged edges in low-resolution lines are known as *aliasing*. This term originated in the field of signal processing and is used to describe problems stemming from low-resolution versions of high-resolution signals. Figure 1.13 is a photograph, taken under a microscope, of such an anti-aliased line on a modern computer screen.

Figure 1.13 An anti-aliased line under a microscope at 20× and 400× magnifications

The left image in figure 1.13 is magnified 20×; the right image, 400×. The rectangular shapes you can see in the images are the separate red, green, and blue sub-pixels, which a modern LCD monitor uses to build up all the different colors and grays it may need (the monitor makes a picture by emitting light and red, green, and blue are the primary colors of light.)

What might a reasonable minimum resolution be? To simplify, let's return to the scenario where we only have black and white dots—no anti-aliasing. The resolution required to make the page look smooth depends on the distance at which the typical viewer sees it. For a computer screen, this might be 20 inches; for a smartphone, 8 inches; and for a billboard, 20 or 50 feet (if you have never walked right up to a billboard and looked at the printing, do so—it is surprisingly coarse.) The limit of the human optical system's ability to distinguish the color of adjacent dots or their existence or absence is the density of light-sensitive cells on the retina. At a distance of 12 inches, a density of 600 dpi on the printed page may be required. For a billboard, we may only need 20 or 50 dpi. On a screen, anti-aliasing allows us to use a lower resolution than we might otherwise need.

1.4   Building shapes

We have seen how to draw lines between points, and so we can build shapes by chaining together multiple lines. For example, the lines $(1, 1)$—$(10, 1)$, $(10, 1)$—$(10, 10)$, $(10, 10)$—$(1, 10)$, and $(1, 10)$—$(1, 1)$ form a square (you can draw it on paper if you wish). We might define this shape more concisely as $(1, 1)$—$(10, 1)$—$(10, 10)$—$(1, 10)$—$(1, 1)$. With this method, we can produce any shape. For example, figure 1.14 shows a child's picture of a house made from several lines.

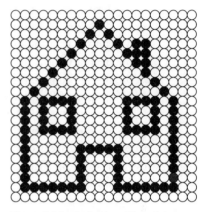

Figure 1.14   A simple outline picture, built from lines

Notice that we have built the image in figure 1.14 using three different sets of joined-up lines: one for the outline of the house and two more, one for each window. Considering the bottom-left dot to be at $(0,0)$, they are, in fact, these sets of lines:

- For the house outline: $(1, 1)$—$(1, 10)$—$(9, 18)$—$(13, 14)$—$(13, 16)$—$(14, 16)$—$(14, 13)$—$(17, 10)$—$(17, 1)$—$(11, 1)$—$(11, 5)$—$(7, 5)$—$(7, 1)$ —$(1, 1)$
- For the left window: $(3, 10)$—$(6, 10)$—$(6, 7)$—$(3, 7)$—$(3, 10)$ $(12, 10)$—$(15, 10)$—$(15, 7)$—$(12, 7)$—$(12, 10)$

We have converted a *vector* graphic (the list of coordinates making up the house) into a *raster* graphic (a set of colors for each dot on the screen or paper).

In this chapter, we have looked at the very basics of how to convert descriptions of shapes into patterns of dots suitable for a printer or screen. We have also explored some of the physical characteristics of screens, paper, and ink. In the next chapter, we will consider the more complicated shapes needed to draw letters and numbers, which consist not only of straight lines but also curves.

NOTE   For suggestions for further reading on the topic covered in this and other chapters, see appendix A.

Problems

For solutions, see appendix B. Templates for you to photocopy or print out for problems 1.2–1.4 are available in appendix C; alternatively, use graph paper or draw your own grids.

1 Give sequences of coordinates that may be used to draw the following sets of lines:

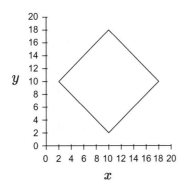 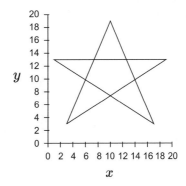

2 Draw the following two sequences of coordinates on separate 20×20 grids, with lines between the points. What do they show?

$(5, 19)$—$(15, 19)$—$(15, 16)$—$(8, 16)$—$(8, 12)$—$(15, 12)$—$(15, 9)$—$(8, 9)$—$(8, 5)$—$(15, 5)$—$(15, 2)$—$(5, 2)$—$(5, 19)$

$(0, 5)$—$(10, 10)$—$(5, 0)$—$(10, 3)$—$(15, 0)$—$(10, 10)$—$(20, 5)$—$(17, 10)$—$(20, 15)$—$(10, 10)$—$(15, 20)$—$(10, 17)$—$(5, \ 20)$—$(10, 10)$—$(0, 15)$—$(3, 10)$—$(0, 5)$

3 Given the following lines on 20×20 grids, select pixels to approximate them.

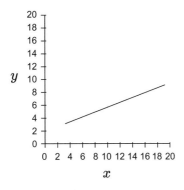 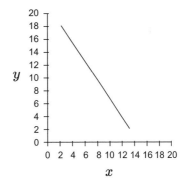

4 On 20×20 grids, choose pixels to fill in to approximate the following characters. Keep them in proportion to one another.

Summary

- This book introduces computer science through eleven little sketches, each related to the theme of book publishing.
- Every page of a book such as this one is made up of a huge number of tiny black ink marks placed onto white paper, or a huge number of pixels, each chosen to be white, black, or gray.
- To make such a page, we have to convert vector descriptions of the shapes (letters and drawings) into raster form.
- There are methods for converting lines to raster form and making shapes from such lines.

Letter forms

This chapter covers

- The mathematics of computer-generated curves
- Building letter outlines from curves
- Drawing filled shapes from outlines

We have learned how to build shapes from straight lines and how to draw those lines onto a screen built from pixels or onto paper using ink. If we only ever drew our shapes at one size, we could just use enough tiny little straight lines to build up any shape, including curved ones. However, we might like to draw our shapes at different sizes or display them on devices with different resolutions (there may be 1,200 dots per inch on a commercial printer, for example, but only 200 dots per inch on a computer screen). We don't really want to store a hundred little lines and their coordinates to describe a circle. We want just to say "a circle of radius 20pt at coordinates (200, 300)," for example. In this chapter, we will learn how to convert descriptions like this into the sets of ink dots or pixels needed to make up an image on paper or screen.

2.1 Straight and curved lines

Consider the shapes that make up a letter of a typeface—*Palatino*, for example, which is described in chapter 9. A typeface is a collection of little shapes, one for each

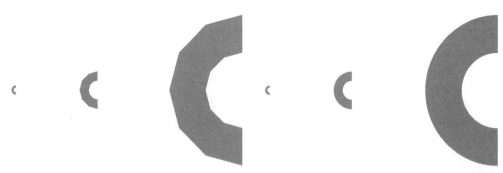

Figure 2.1   The letter C composed of only straight lines

Figure 2.2   The letter C composed of only straight lines and circular arcs

letter, that are arranged on the page in lines. We must be able to scale them to different sizes (for example, large for chapter headings and smaller for footnotes). They most often contain curves as well as straight lines. Consider the letter C, which has curved parts. Figure 2.1 shows the effect of increasing the size of a letter C designed using only lines. Figure 2.2 shows how we could use these sections of circles (or arcs) to build our letter C instead.

In figure 2.1, the straight lines survive scaling intact, but the curves are spoiled. Almost as simple as drawing lines (at least on paper) is drawing circles. We can do this with a pair of compasses (figure 2.2). However, this method suffices only for simple letter forms. Imagine trying to draw complicated curves, such as the ampersand character, as shown in figure 2.3, using just a pair of compasses.

Figure 2.3   A letter shape requiring many curves

Circular arcs don't help much here (not every curve is part of a circle). We would need dozens of, if not a hundred, pieces of circles to accurately follow the shape of the letter. Before computers, the solution was a set of *French curves,* which are shaped pieces of wood, rubber, or plastic whose contours are composed of curves of varying tightness. Figure 2.4 shows a typical set of French curves. The curves are manipulated by moving and rotating them until an appropriate contour is found for part of the desired shape. Sometimes this is done by starting with points through which the curve must pass, making it easier to line up the forms. A complex curve will be made up of several different parts of the French curves, making sure that the joins between the chosen sections are smooth.

The curve sections used and points passed through can be recorded so that the shape may be reproduced. Such curves are no longer used by drafters, who use computers instead, but they are still used by, for example, dressmakers. A larger, less tightly curved set of shapes were formerly used for the design of boat hulls. They are known as *ship curves.*

Figure 2.4   French curves

2.2   *Computerized curves*

How might we apply these techniques to computerized drawing? Two Frenchmen in the car industry, Pierre Bézier (1910–1999) at Renault and Paul de Casteljau (1930–2022) at Citroën, are responsible for the development of a kind of curve that is easy and predictable for the designer to work with, can be used to describe many useful sorts of shapes, and is amenable to manipulation and display by computer. They are known as *Bézier curves*.

We have seen that a straight line may be defined simply by its two endpoints—for example, (1, 3)—(6, 5). A Bézier curve is defined by four points: its two endpoints and two other points called *control points*, one for each endpoint. These control points, which may be positioned anywhere, are used to pull the curve away from the straight line between the endpoints. The further away the control points are, the more the curve deviates from the straight line between its endpoints. Figure 2.5 shows several Bézier curves. (The control points are shown linked to their respective endpoints with dotted lines.)

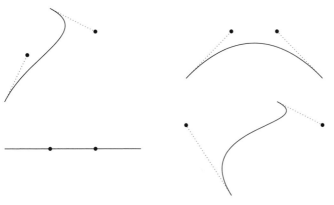

Figure 2.5   Several Bézier curves and their control points (shown as black dots)

Note that a Bézier curve may bend one or two ways; it may also be straight. The designer can move the control points interactively to build a wide range of curved lines. If you have access to an interactive graphics program on your computer, try using it to play with the control points of a Bézier curve.

The curves we have made are still too simple to build a complicated shape, such as our ampersand. To make such shapes, we stitch together a number of such curves, making sure that an endpoint of one curve coincides with an endpoint of the next, forming a chain. Figure 2.6 shows a set of such chains for our ampersand. There are three chains of curves, which we call *paths*, in the ampersand: one for the main shape and two others—one for each of the "holes." There are 58 curves, of which 5 are straight lines.

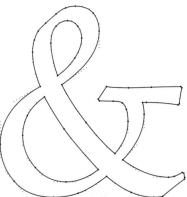

Figure 2.6   Three Bézier curve chains (paths) used to draw an ampersand character

Note that several of these curves join very smoothly to one another. This is a matter of getting the control points for both curves in the right place: if the control point associated with the endpoint of one curve is arranged at 180° to the control point associated with the endpoint of the next, the join will be smooth, with no change in slope at that point. Otherwise, there will be a definite corner. If the endpoints of two adjacent curves in the sequence do not coincide at all, there will be a gap. (We call such curves *discontinuous*.) Figure 2.7 gives examples of discontinuous, continuous, and smooth continuous Bézier curve pairs.

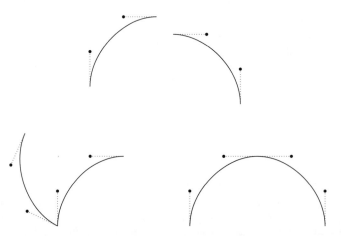

Figure 2.7   Discontinuous (upper), continuous (lower left), and smooth continuous (lower right) pairs of Bézier curves. Notice the control points in the smooth continuous case are at 180° to one another.

How can we draw a Bézier curve on the screen or print it on paper? It seems much more complicated than the straight lines we have already drawn. It turns out, though, that there is a simple way: we repeatedly split up the curve into smaller and smaller sections until each one is almost as flat as a line. Then, we can draw each of those little lines using the method we developed in chapter 1. How do we perform such a subdivision? We could pick equally spaced points along the length of the curve. However, this approach would use too many lines where the curve is open and too few when the curve is tight.

An algorithm (method), devised by De Casteljau, is simple enough to do on paper and produces a subdivision of the curve that is appropriate to the tightness of each part. Consider the curve with endpoints A and D and control points B and C shown at the top left of figure 2.8.

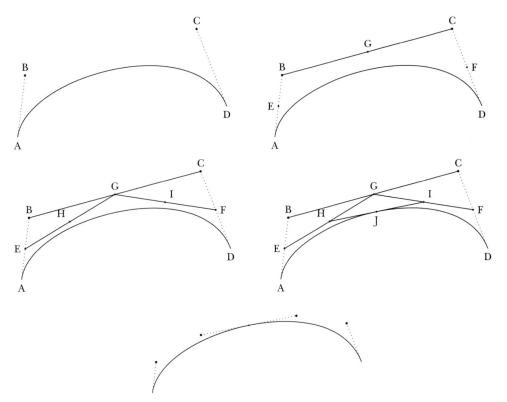

Figure 2.8   De Casteljau curve subdivision

At the top right of figure 2.8, the halfway points E and F have been drawn on the lines between the endpoints and control points and point G halfway between the control points. Now, we draw lines between points E and G and between points F and G and find the halfway points H and I on those lines (middle-left diagram). Halfway between those is point J, which is the mid-point of the original curve and the endpoint of both new curves we are creating (middle-right diagram). The two final curves can now be seen: AEHJ and JIFD. They are shown on their own in the bottom diagram.

This procedure works for any Bézier curve. We can proceed to subdivide each of these smaller curves. Once we have subdivided enough times, each of the little curves should

Figure 2.9   A Bézier curve approximated by 1, 2, 4, 6, 7, 10, 13, 21, and 25 straight lines

be flat enough to be roughly equivalent to a straight line between its endpoints. So we can just draw each as a straight line using the procedure described in chapter 1.

How do we decide when to stop the subdivision? If we stop after a fixed number of stages, the difference between the treatment of open and tight parts of the curve again becomes apparent. Instead, we calculate a crude measure of the flatness of a curve and finish when it is less than a certain amount (say, half the width of a pixel). A line is then an appropriate substitute for that curve. Figure 2.9 shows a Bézier curve approximated by 1, 2, 4, 6, 7, 10, 13, 21, and 25 straight lines as a result of repeated application of de Casteljau's procedure, stopping when each section is flat enough according to such a test.

Figure 2.10 shows one such approximate measure of flatness, which is relatively easy to calculate: the height of the curve. If the length $A + B$ is less than a given small number, we can approximate the curve with a line. This length will always be greater than the maximum deviation of the curve from the straight line joining its endpoints.

2.3   *Complications*

We rejected the use of circular arcs due to their inflexibility, replacing them with Bézier curves, but there is an irony: no combination of Bézier curves can exactly represent a circle or circular arc. However, we can get close enough. For a full circle, four Bézier curves will get us there. Figure 2.11 shows

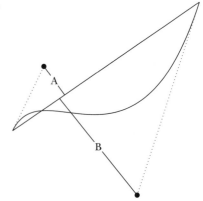

Figure 2.10   An approximate measure of the flatness of a Bézier curve

circles built from two and four Bézier curves. Can you see the difference between the two circles?

There is a further complication: How do we draw a letter that has a hole in it—for example, the letter O? As shown in figure 2.11, we simply use two discontinuous paths—one for the outer circle and one for the inner. In the previous chapter, we looked at a simple way to fill closed shapes like the one. Let's formalize our method a little. When we fill such a shape, we fill any part where a line from that point to somewhere outside the letter crosses the shape an odd number of times. So, for our letter O, the inside path is not filled, as required. This is known as the *even–odd* filling rule.

In figure 2.12, we used a sloped line to count the crossings, whereas in the previous chapter, we followed a horizontal row of pixels. It doesn't really matter: the result is the same. We don't paint points in the middle of the O because there are two

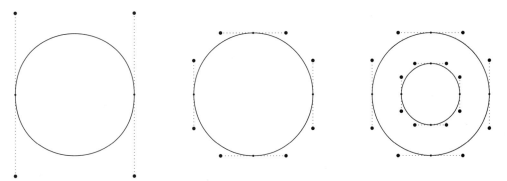

Figure 2.11   **Circles built from two and four Bézier curves and a letter with a hole in it formed from two such circles**

crossings between there and outside the shape, and two is an even number. However, the even–odd method does not suffice when the path crosses itself. For example, consider the self-crossing path in figure 2.13: our even–odd method gives a peculiar and unwanted result.

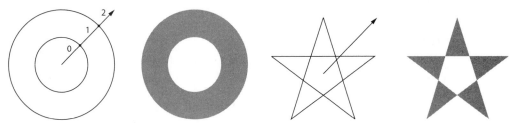

Figure 2.12   **The even–odd filling rule**

Figure 2.13   **The even–odd filling rule on a self-crossing path**

We can remedy this odd result by changing the rule: now we will look at the direction of the path at each point, counting 1 for each clockwise and –1 for each anti-clockwise crossing. We fill if the number is nonzero, and the result is the one we want, as shown in figure 2.14.

Our line crosses two anti-clockwise lines and is therefore nonzero (it has a count of 0 – 1 – 1, which is –2). We can apply this rule to our O example, but there is a problem: the inner hole is also filled, as shown in figure 2.15.

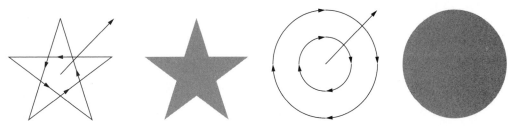

Figure 2.14   **The nonzero filling rule**

Figure 2.15   **The nonzero filling rule for our letter O**

This filling of the inner hole, as shown in figure 2.15, can be fixed by reversing the direction of either of the two paths. We now have a method that works for both cases, as shown in figure 2.16.

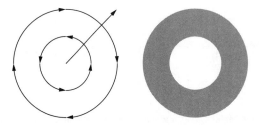

Figure 2.16   **Reversing the path order with the nonzero filling rule**

The methods described in this chapter are followed automatically thousands of times a second when an eBook page is viewed or when a book is printed. This ability to follow complex instructions quickly and repeatedly shows the power of computers to release us from labor. Now that we have some understanding of how to draw lines and curves on paper or the screen, we will turn to the input, storage, and manipulation of the text itself before returning to the visual layout of the page later in the book.

Problems

For solutions, see appendix B. A template for you to photocopy or print out for problem 2.1 is available in appendix C.

1 Print out or trace the following Bézier curve, and divide it into two using the procedure of De Casteljau. You will need a pencil and a ruler.

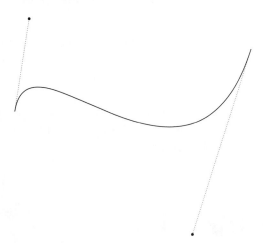

2 If you have access to a computer, find a drawing program with Bézier curves and experiment to gain an intuitive understanding of how they are manipulated. At the time of writing, one such free program is Inkscape, suitable for most computers.

3 Fill in the following shapes using the even–odd filling rule and again using the non-zero filling rule. The direction of each line is indicated by the little arrows. The second and third pictures contain two separate, overlapping square paths.

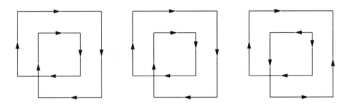

Summary

- When computers draw curves on the screen or on paper, they are really just drawing lots of tiny straight lines. The straight lines are calculated by subdivision of the curve.
- We can link curves together to design letter forms for each character and so draw them on the page. Each page of a book contains thousands of such curves.
- Filling a letter shape can be more complicated than it looks, especially when the shape of the letter has a hole in it.

Storing words

This chapter covers

- Representing letters as numbers so computers can process them
- Working with text formatting such as bold and italic
- The Unicode™ standard for the world's languages and writing systems

We have added lines and curves to our repertoire in the previous chapter. Now let's look at storing and manipulating text.

Computers deal only in numbers. These numbers are processed in various ways, with no particular meaning assigned to them. However, we like to assign meaning, so we use a code to say which number means what. For example, we might set 0 = A, 1 = B, 2 = C, etc. This code exists only in our heads and our computer programs— the computer itself still sees just numbers. From the very beginning, computers have been used to process textual data, to have textual input (from keyboards and similar devices), and to have textual output (to line printers, which were a little like a conventional typewriter but connected to a computer rather than a typist's keyboard). The descendants of these coding and decoding mechanisms are still in use today: they are our computer keyboards and mice and our mobile phone or tablet touchscreens. In this chapter, we will look at some of the ancient and modern ways to encode text as numbers.

3.1   Ancient methods

Methods of encoding letters as numbers for communication have ancient origins. The Greek historian Polybius
(c. 118 BC–c. 200 BC) relates a number of methods of
communication in *The Histories*, including his own based
on fire signals. The 24 letters of the Greek alphabet
would be placed in a grid and reduced in this way to two
numbers between 1 and 5 (the coordinates of the number in the grid). Figure 3.1 shows such a grid for English
(I and J must share a slot since we have 26 letters).

	1	2	3	4	5
1	A	B	C	D	E
2	F	G	H	I/J	K
3	L	M	N	O	P
4	Q	R	S	T	U
5	V	W	X	Y	Z

Figure 3.1   A grid for English letters

Now we can signal a letter using just two numbers,
each between 1 and 5. For example, the word POLYBIUS, taking row first and column
second, is 35–34–31–54–12–24–45–43. That is to say, P is at row 3, column 5, and so on.
Now, to transmit a letter, we need only transmit two small numbers. Polybius's system
used two banks of five torches. For P, we would set three torches to the up position on
the left and five on the right. The recipient would then set his torches the same way to
acknowledge receipt.

3.2   Numbers in computing

Computers, however, do not deal in 5s or, indeed, in the 10s and 100s we do ordinary
mathematics in. At the lowest level, we do not have 10 or 5 things to choose from,
but just 2: on and off, yes and no, the presence of electricity or its absence. However,
computers can store and process millions or billions of such numbers. They are known
as *bits*, and a bit is either off or on. We use the familiar digits 0 and 1 to represent them:
0 for off and 1 for on. If we are to represent letters using only 1 bit, we don't have many,
as shown in figure 3.2. Luckily, since we have billions of such bits, we can use more for
each letter. When we add a bit, we double the number of bit combinations and thus the
number of representable letters. Now we have four, as shown in figure 3.3.

Bits	Number represented	Letter represented
0	0	A
1	1	B

Figure 3.2   One bit represents only two letters.

Bits	Number	Letter
00	0	A
01	1	B
10	2	C
11	3	D

Figure 3.3   Two bits represent four letters.

Add another bit, and we have eight, as shown in figure 3.4. If we use 8 bits, we have 256
slots available, from 0 to 255, which is enough, at least for all the usual characters and
symbols in English, as shown in figure 3.5. These 8-bit groups are very common, so they
have a special name. We call them *bytes*. In fact, we normally talk about something being
150 bytes in size, for example, rather than 1,200 bits.

Bits	Number	Letter
000	0	A
001	1	B
010	2	C
011	3	D
100	4	E
101	5	F
110	6	G
111	7	H

Figure 3.4 Letters with 3 bits

Bits	Number
00000000	0
00000001	1
00000010	2
00000011	3
:	:
11111100	252
11111101	253
11111110	254
11111111	255

Figure 3.5 Eight bits can represent 256 different things.

The representations of these numbers using just 0 and 1 are simply base-2 (binary) arithmetic rather than our usual base-10 (decimal) arithmetic. Just as base-10 126 is $1 \times 100 + 2 \times 10 + 6 \times 1$, so base-2 101 in figure 3.4 is $1 \times 4 + 0 \times 2 + 1 \times 1$. In this book, however, we will not need such arithmetic explicitly.

In the early days of computers, in the mid-20th century, each organization building a computer would design it mostly from scratch with little regard for interoperability (that is, the ability for computers to talk to one another using the same codes). Since they might have been building the only computer in their country at the time, interoperability was hardly a concern. Due to the size of the memory in these machines and the characteristics of their design, the number of characters easily and efficiently represented was often small. For example, there may have been only 64 slots. There may not even be enough space for both uppercase and lowercase letters! There had been standardized codes before, of course, for telegraph communication, but they were largely disregarded. Let's take as an example the code used in the EDSAC (Electronic Delay Storage Automatic Calculator) computer at the University of Cambridge, which was built between 1946 and 1949. There were two sets of 32 characters (the "letter set"), each represented by the numbers 0 to 31 (the "figure set"). Two of the characters were reserved for switching (or "shifting") between the two sets. This is rather like the shift key that we still use on keyboards today to avoid having to have two sets of keys (one for lowercase and one for uppercase). The arrangement is shown in figure 3.6.

In these tables, *figs* and *lets* are the letter and figure shifts. The *cr* and *lf* characters (as we will see) are for moving the printing position around. The *null* character is often used for demarcation purposes (for example, to denote the end of a sequence of things). Notice that the letters are not in order and there are no lowercase letters.

Letter set | | | | | | Figure set

0	P	8	I	16	null	24	lf		0	0	8	8	16	null	24	lf
1	Q	9	O	17	F	25	L		1	1	9	9	17	$	25	)
2	W	10	J	18	cr	26	X		2	2	10	?	18	cr	26	/
3	E	11	figs	19	D	27	G		3	3	11	figs	19	;	27	#
4	R	12	S	20	space	28	A		4	4	12	"	20	space	28	-
5	T	13	Z	21	H	29	B		5	5	13	+	21	£	29	?
6	Y	14	K	22	N	30	C		6	6	14	(	22	,	30	:
7	U	15	lets	23	M	31	V		7	7	15	lets	23	.	31	=

Figure 3.6   EDSAC's letter and figure sets

3.3   *An international standard*

So that computers may talk to each other and the same program might run on different kinds of computers, standard codes have been developed. Figure 3.7 shows the
ASCII (American Standard Code for Information Interchange) code, defined by an
international consortium in the 1960s.

0	NUL	16	DLE	32	space	48	0	64	@	80	P	96	`	112	p
1	SOH	17	DC1	33	!	49	1	65	A	81	Q	97	a	113	q
2	STX	18	DC2	34	"	50	2	66	B	82	R	98	b	114	r
3	ETX	19	DC3	35	#	51	3	67	C	83	S	99	c	115	s
4	EOT	20	DC4	36	$	52	4	68	D	84	T	100	d	116	t
5	ENQ	21	NAK	37	%	53	5	69	E	85	U	101	e	117	u
6	ACK	22	SYN	38	&	54	6	70	F	86	V	102	f	118	v
7	BEL	23	ETB	39	'	55	7	71	G	87	W	103	g	119	w
8	BS	24	CAN	40	(	56	8	72	H	88	X	104	h	120	x
9	TAB	25	EM	41	)	57	9	73	I	89	Y	105	i	121	y
10	LF	26	SUB	42	*	58	:	74	J	90	Z	106	j	122	z
11	VT	27	ESC	43	+	59	;	75	K	91	[	107	k	123	{
12	FF	28	FS	44	,	60	<	76	L	92	\	108	l	124	|
13	CR	29	GS	45	-	61	=	77	M	93	]	109	m	125	}
14	SO	30	RS	46	.	62	>	78	N	94	^	110	n	126	~
15	SI	31	US	47	/	63	?	79	O	95	_	111	o	127	DEL

Figure 3.7   The ASCII code

Some of these numbers represent real, printable characters, such as 65 for A. Others
represent special codes, such as 13 for CR, which means *carriage return* and originally
referred to the carriage of a typewriter-like device returning to the beginning of the line.
Character 10 for LF, which means *line feed*, refers to a similar device shifting the paper
up one line, so we may begin printing the next. The space character 32 moves one
space across without printing anything. Most of the other special codes are of historical

interest only. We can work out the ASCII codes to represent a piece of text by looking at each character and finding its number in the table. Consider this quotation:

```
"It's the oldest question of all George.
 Who can spy on the spies?"
  -- John Le Carre, "Tinker Tailor Soldier Spy"
```

Notice that we do not have the acute accent for the e in Le Carré's name, and we have to use two dashes – to make what would normally be the – long dash. There must be a carriage return, followed by a line feed at the end of each line to move the printing position to the beginning of the next line. We obtain the sequence of numbers shown in figure 3.8.

"	34	t	116	space	32	p	112	space	32	l	108
I	73	i	105	w	119	i	105	C	67	o	111
t	116	o	111	h	104	e	101	a	97	r	114
'	39	n	110	o	111	s	115	r	114	,	44
s	115	space	32	space	32	?	63	r	114	space	32
space	32	o	111	c	99	"	34	e	101	S	83
t	116	f	102	a	97	cr	13	,	44	o	111
h	104	space	32	n	110	lf	10	space	32	l	108
e	101	a	97	space	32	space	32	"	34	d	100
space	32	l	108	s	115	space	32	T	84	i	105
o	111	l	108	p	112	space	32	i	105	e	101
l	108	space	32	y	121	-	45	n	110	r	114
d	100	G	71	space	32	-	45	n	110	,	44
e	101	e	101	o	111	space	32	k	107	space	32
s	115	o	111	n	110	J	74	e	101	S	83
t	116	r	114	space	32	o	111	r	114	p	112
space	32	g	103	t	116	h	104	,	44	y	121
q	113	e	101	h	104	n	110	space	32	"	34
u	117	.	46	e	101	space	32	T	84		
e	101	cr	13	space	32	L	76	a	97		
s	115	lf	10	s	115	e	101	i	105		

Figure 3.8   ASCII codes for each letter in our quotation

There are many more characters in the world than these and, therefore, many standards for extending this table. These standards include the addition of accented characters in the Western languages and the use of other methods altogether for the world's other character sets—for example, the Cyrillic characters of Russian, the Han characters of Chinese, and the many writing methods of languages from the Indian subcontinent. We will examine one of these standards later in this chapter.

3.4 Formatting

We have seen how the carriage return and line feed characters may be used to change the way our text is laid out (sometimes called *formatting*). However, we have not seen how to change the typeface, *type shape*, **type thickness**, or the size of the text. We should like to be able to introduce such changes during the run of the text, as in this paragraph. What is needed is a way to "mark up" the text with annotations such as "make this word bold" or "change to type size 8pt here." Such methods are known as *markup languages*.

We could imagine a system where typing, for example, "`This *word* must be bold`" into the computer would produce "This **word** must be bold" on the printed page or electronic document. We could use a symbol for each other kind of change—for example, `$` for italic—so we can write "`$awful$`" and get "*awful*." A problem arises, though. What if we wish to type a literal `$` character? We must escape the clutches of the special formatting symbols temporarily. We do so using what is called an *escape character*. The most common is `\` (the backslash). We say that any character immediately following the escape character is to be rendered literally. So, we can write "`And $especially$ for \$10`" to produce "And *especially* for $10". How then do we type a backslash itself? Well, the backslash can escape itself just as well! We simply write `\\`. So, the literal text "`The \\ character`" produces "The \ character."

Let's look at how some common markup systems represent the following piece of formatted text:

Section Title

This is the *first* paragraph, which is **important**.

We might, for example, extend our system of special characters in the following fashion:

```
!Section Title!
This is the $first$ paragraph, which is *important*.
```

In the language used for web pages, HyperText Markup Language (HTML), the starting and ending signifiers, called *tags*, are not symmetrical. A tag such as `<b>` begins bold, and the tag `</b>` ends it. We can also use `<i>` and `</i>` for italic, `<h1>` and `</h1>` for the heading, and `<p>` and `</p>` to explicitly mark paragraphs. (In the previous method, we had just used carriage returns and line feeds to mark them.) We may write:

```
<h1>Section Title</h1>
<p>This is the <i>first</i>, which is <b>important</b>.</p>
```

In the typesetting language used for writing this book, markup is introduced with the backslash escape character, followed by a descriptive name of the change being made, with the contents enclosed in curly brackets { and }:

```
\section{Section Title}
This is the \textit{first} paragraph, which is \textbf{important}.
```

Here, we have used \section{} for the section title, \textit{} for italic, and \textbf{} for bold. These differing markup systems are not just historical artifacts: they serve different purposes. The requirements may be wholly different for a document to be printed, to be put on the web, or to be viewed on an eBook reader.

3.5   *Modern encoding systems*

Since 1989, there has been an international industrial effort, under the Unicode initiative, to encode more than 100,000 characters, giving each a number and defining how they may be combined in valid ways. More than 1 million total slots are available for future use. Importantly, the Unicode system is concerned only with assigning characters to numbers. It does not specify the shapes those characters take: that is a matter for typeface designers. The principle is one of separation of concerns: each part of a computer system should do one job well and allow interaction with the other, similarly well-designed components. This separation of concerns is particularly difficult for the Unicode system, which must navigate innumerable cultural differences and a wide variety of possible uses.

The following figures show some examples drawn from the huge Unicode standard. Figure 3.9 shows the ASCII characters we have already seen. They appear in the same places as in the ASCII standard—that is, if ASCII uses a particular number for the letter A, for example, so does the Unicode assignment (in the figure, the base-16 number 0041 shown is equal to the decimal number 65 ASCII uses for the letter A). This is called *backward compatibility* and is hugely important in helping computer systems continue to fit together over multidecade timescales.

Figure 3.10 shows the Western accented characters and common symbols. It is a subset of the common symbols and accented letters used in Western languages. Notice that some of the letters come with their accents attached, but some (for example, the cedilla in column 00B, row 8) are made to be attached to several letters. Again, this discussion is for historical reasons: for many years, it was not clear which was the best approach, and now the two must sit alongside one another. Such complexity is the disadvantage of backward compatibility.

Figure 3.11 shows the Thai alphabet. Consonants are written left to right, with vowels arranged around them. The vowels are the characters in the table with little dotted circles. The dotted circle is not visible: it indicates the relative position of the consonant and vowel when the two are combined. This table is directly included in the Unicode standard from the existing Thai Industrial Standard (TIS-620), simply with the numbers shifted. The Unicode system tries to do this whenever possible for some level of backward compatibility.

Figure 3.12 shows Braille patterns. The top section contains all those combinations using the top six dots only. (There were originally only six dots in Braille.) All the others then follow, for a total of 256. The patterns are not assigned particular letters because these vary for each language: a pattern might represent the letter A in Western languages and something entirely different in Japanese or Vietnamese. Empty circles

	000	001	002	003	004	005	006	007
0	NUL 0000	DLE 0010	SP 0020	0 0030	@ 0040	P 0050	` 0060	p 0070
1	SOH 0001	DC1 0011	! 0021	1 0031	A 0041	Q 0051	a 0061	q 0071
2	STX 0002	DC2 0012	" 0022	2 0032	B 0042	R 0052	b 0062	r 0072
3	ETX 0003	DC3 0013	# 0023	3 0033	C 0043	S 0053	c 0063	s 0073
4	EOT 0004	DC4 0014	$ 0024	4 0034	D 0044	T 0054	d 0064	t 0074
5	ENQ 0005	NAK 0015	% 0025	5 0035	E 0045	U 0055	e 0065	u 0075
6	ACK 0006	SYN 0016	& 0026	6 0036	F 0046	V 0056	f 0066	v 0076
7	BEL 0007	ETB 0017	' 0027	7 0037	G 0047	W 0057	g 0067	w 0077
8	BS 0008	CAN 0018	(0028	8 0038	H 0048	X 0058	h 0068	x 0078
9	HT 0009	EM 0019	) 0029	9 0039	I 0049	Y 0059	i 0069	y 0079
A	LF 000A	SUB 001A	* 002A	: 003A	J 004A	Z 005A	j 006A	z 007A
B	VT 000B	ESC 001B	+ 002B	; 003B	K 004B	[005B	k 006B	{ 007B
C	FF 000C	FS 001C	, 002C	< 003C	L 004C	\ 005C	l 006C	| 007C
D	CR 000D	GS 001D	- 002D	= 003D	M 004D	] 005D	m 006D	} 007D
E	SO 000E	RS 001E	. 002E	> 003E	N 004E	^ 005E	n 006E	~ 007E
F	SI 000F	US 001F	/ 002F	? 003F	O 004F	_ 005F	o 006F	DEL 007F

Figure 3.9   Unicode table showing ASCII characters. (Unicode and the Unicode Logo are registered trademarks of Unicode, Inc. in the United States and other countries)

	008	009	00A	00B	00C	00D	00E	00F
0	XXX 0080	DCS 0090	NB SP 00A0	° 00B0	À 00C0	Ð 00D0	à 00E0	ð 00F0
1	XXX 0081	PU1 0091	¡ 00A1	± 00B1	Á 00C1	Ñ 00D1	á 00E1	ñ 00F1
2	BPH 0082	PU2 0092	¢ 00A2	² 00B2	Â 00C2	Ò 00D2	â 00E2	ò 00F2
3	NBH 0083	STS 0093	£ 00A3	³ 00B3	Ã 00C3	Ó 00D3	ã 00E3	ó 00F3
4	IND 0084	CCH 0094	¤ 00A4	´ 00B4	Ä 00C4	Ô 00D4	ä 00E4	ô 00F4
5	NEL 0085	MW 0095	¥ 00A5	µ 00B5	Å 00C5	Õ 00D5	å 00E5	õ 00F5
6	SSA 0086	SPA 0096	¦ 00A6	¶ 00B6	Æ 00C6	Ö 00D6	æ 00E6	ö 00F6
7	ESA 0087	EPA 0097	§ 00A7	· 00B7	Ç 00C7	× 00D7	ç 00E7	÷ 00F7
8	HTS 0088	SOS 0098	¨ 00A8	¸ 00B8	È 00C8	Ø 00D8	è 00E8	ø 00F8
9	HTJ 0089	XXX 0099	© 00A9	¹ 00B9	É 00C9	Ù 00D9	é 00E9	ù 00F9
A	VTS 008A	SCI 009A	ª 00AA	º 00BA	Ê 00CA	Ú 00DA	ê 00EA	ú 00FA
B	PLD 008B	CSI 009B	« 00AB	» 00BB	Ë 00CB	Û 00DB	ë 00EB	û 00FB
C	PLU 008C	ST 009C	¬ 00AC	¼ 00BC	Ì 00CC	Ü 00DC	ì 00EC	ü 00FC
D	RI 008D	OSC 009D	SHY 00AD	½ 00BD	Í 00CD	Ý 00DD	í 00ED	ý 00FD
E	SS2 008E	PM 009E	® 00AE	¾ 00BE	Î 00CE	Þ 00DE	î 00EE	þ 00FE
F	SS3 008F	APC 009F	¯ 00AF	¿ 00BF	Ï 00CF	ß 00DF	ï 00EF	ÿ 00FF

Figure 3.10   Western accented characters and common symbols

Figure 3.11   The Thai alphabet

	280	281	282	283	284	285	286	287	288	289	28A	28B	28C	28D	28E	28F
0	2800	2810	2820	2830	2840	2850	2860	2870	2880	2890	28A0	28B0	28C0	28D0	28E0	28F0
1	2801	2811	2821	2831	2841	2851	2861	2871	2881	2891	28A1	28B1	28C1	28D1	28E1	28F1
2	2802	2812	2822	2832	2842	2852	2862	2872	2882	2892	28A2	28B2	28C2	28D2	28E2	28F2
3	2803	2813	2823	2833	2843	2853	2863	2873	2883	2893	28A3	28B3	28C3	28D3	28E3	28F3
4	2804	2814	2824	2834	2844	2854	2864	2874	2884	2894	28A4	28B4	28C4	28D4	28E4	28F4
5	2805	2815	2825	2835	2845	2855	2865	2875	2885	2895	28A5	28B5	28C5	28D5	28E5	28F5
6	2806	2816	2826	2836	2846	2856	2866	2876	2886	2896	28A6	28B6	28C6	28D6	28E6	28F6
7	2807	2817	2827	2837	2847	2857	2867	2877	2887	2897	28A7	28B7	28C7	28D7	28E7	28F7
8	2808	2818	2828	2838	2848	2858	2868	2878	2888	2898	28A8	28B8	28C8	28D8	28E8	28F8
9	2809	2819	2829	2839	2849	2859	2869	2879	2889	2899	28A9	28B9	28C9	28D9	28E9	28F9
A	280A	281A	282A	283A	284A	285A	286A	287A	288A	289A	28AA	28BA	28CA	28DA	28EA	28FA
B	280B	281B	282B	283B	284B	285B	286B	287B	288B	289B	28AB	28BB	28CB	28DB	28EB	28FB
C	280C	281C	282C	283C	284C	285C	286C	287C	288C	289C	28AC	28BC	28CC	28DC	28EC	28FC
D	280D	281D	282D	283D	284D	285D	286D	287D	288D	289D	28AD	28BD	28CD	28DD	28ED	28FD
E	280E	281E	282E	283E	284E	285E	286E	287E	288E	289E	28AE	28BE	28CE	28DE	28EE	28FE
F	280F	281F	282F	283F	284F	285F	286F	287F	288F	289F	28AF	28BF	28CF	28DF	28EF	28FF

Figure 3.12   Braille patterns

Figure 3.13   Linear A

are used in most Braille typefaces so that, in patterns with only a few black dots, the empty circles can be felt with the finger to help distinguish between different characters. This is particularly useful when dealing with eight-dot patterns.

Figure 3.13 shows Linear A, an undeciphered writing system of ancient Greece, thought to have been in use 2500–1400 BC. It was added to the Unicode specification in 2014. We do not need to understand a writing system to reproduce it electronically! Most specimens were found on Crete, although they have been found as far apart as Bulgaria and Israel.

In the next chapter, we will see how to process text already in the computer by searching.

Problems

For solutions, see appendix B.

1 Using the method of Polybius, encode the phrase "MARYHADALITTLELAMB." How many characters are in the message? How many numbers are needed to encode them? Can you think of a way to indicate the concept of "end of message" in Polybius's system? What about spaces?

2 Complete a table of bits, numbers, and letters for a system that uses 5 bits for each character. How many lines does the table have? Which characters did you deem important enough to include?

3 Decode the following message from ASCII: 84 114 101 97 115 111 110 105 115 118 101 114 121 109 117 99 104 97 109 97 116 116 101 114 111 102 104 97 98 105 116 44 83 109 105 108 101 121 100 101 99 105 100 101 100 46.

4 Encode the following message from *Tinker Tailor Soldier Spy* into ASCII: The more identities a man has, the more they express the person they conceal.

5 In a markup language in which \ is the escape character, a pair of $s around a word means *italic*, and a pair of *s around a word mean **bold**, give the marked-up text for the following literal pieces of text:

The love of money is the root of **all** evil.
The love of $$$ is the root of all evil.
The love of *$$$* is the root of all evil.
The love of **$$$** is the root of all evil.

Summary

- The characters we use to make up our words and sentences are represented by numbers inside the computer.
- Characters have been encoded into numbers since ancient times.
- In the early days of computers, simple encodings containing no more than 128 characters were used, such as ASCII.
- Today, we use Unicode, which aims to represent the world's writing systems in one unified encoding.

- Markup languages allow us to add annotations to text to control changes to the typeface, such as bold or italics.
- Different markup languages serve different purposes, with varying requirements depending on whether the output is for print, web, or an eBook.

Looking and finding 4

This chapter covers

- How computer programs are made
- Building a simple computer program for searching
- Measuring and improving a program's speed

When writing a book, it is important to be able to efficiently wrangle a long piece of text. One important task is to search for a word, finding where it has been used. We may then jump to such a position in the text, see what is around the word, and modify or replace it. We need to do this on demand, without an explicitly prepared index. In fact, we have indexes at the back of books because searching through the book manually, from front to back, is slow and error prone for a human. Luckily, it is fast and accurate for a computer. In this chapter, we will learn how to write a computer program to search text and then improve it to measure and increase the search speed.

4.1 A simple method

It might seem that it is easy to describe to a computer how to search for a word: just look for it! But we must prepare an explicit method, made of tiny little simple steps for the computer to follow. Everything must be explained in perfect detail—no big assumptions, no hand waving. Such a careful, explicit method is called an *algorithm*.

What are the basic operations from which we can build such an algorithm? Assume we have the text to be searched and the word to search for at hand. Each of them is made up of *characters* (A, x, ! etc.). Assume also that we know how to compare two characters to see whether they are alike or different. For example, A is the same as A but different from B. Let's pick a concrete example: we will try to find the word `horses` in the text `houses and horses and hearses`. Let's number each of the 29 characters in the text and the 6 characters in the word:

```
          1         2
T 012345678901234567890123456789
  houses and horses and hearses


W 012345
  horses
```

We have called the text `T` and the word `W`. Notice that we number upward from 0, not 1. This is a common convention in computing. Let's begin by describing a simple searching method and then refine it into smaller steps. We will be answering the question "Does the word appear in the text and, if so, where?" The answer will be a series of 0, 1, or more numbers giving the matching positions. Let's compare positions 0 to 5 in `W` with positions 0 to 5 in `T`. Plainly, they do not all match, although some of them do. Position 2 differs (`r` in the word `W` but `u` in the text `T`), which is enough to declare failure. Now, we will shift the whole word `W` one position and try again:

```
          1         2
T 012345678901234567890123456789
  houses and horses and hearses


W  012345
   horses
```

Here, we fail on every character in our comparison. And we keep failing again and again at each position we try, moving rightward one each time:

```
          1         2
T 012345678901234567890123456789
  houses and horses and hearses


W           012345
            horses
```

Finally, though, we find the match (every character is the same), and we can declare that the word `W` is found at position 11 in the text `T`:

```
          1         2
T 012345678901234567890123456789
  houses and horses and hearses


W           012345
            horses
```

If we reach a situation where the word overruns the end of the text, we stop immediately—no further match can now be found:

```
          1         2
T 012345678901234567890012345678
  houses and horses and hearses

W                       012345
                        horses
```

We have worked out our method in detail, describing it in words and diagrams with reasonable formality. But computers require unreasonable formality: a set of instructions written in a programming language that describes the algorithm exactly, not loosely or even almost exactly.

4.2   Writing a program

Let's try to write our algorithm out as a computer program. A program is a set of instructions written in a language that is understandable and unambiguous, both to the computer and to the human being writing it. First, we will assume that the part of the program for comparing the word with the text at a given position already exists: we will write it later. For now, we will concentrate on the part that decides where to start and stop, moves the word along the text position by position, and prints out any positions that match. For reasons of conciseness, we won't use a real programming language but a *pseudocode*—that is, a language that closely resembles any number of programming languages but contains only the complexities needed for describing the solution to our particular problem. First, we define a new algorithm called search, as shown in the following listing.

Listing 4.1   **Starting our algorithm**

```
1 define search pt
```

We use the *keyword* **define** to say that we are defining a new algorithm (keywords are built into the programming language, and we write them in bold). Then, we give our algorithm the name search. (This is arbitrary; we could call it fred if we want.) We give the name of the thing this algorithm will work with, called a *parameter*—in our case, pt, which will be a number that tracks how far along in the searching process we are (pt for *position* in *text*). We will arrange for the value of pt to begin at 0, the first character. Our algorithm doesn't do anything yet. If we asked the computer to run it, nothing would happen.

Now, we want to make sure that we do not overrun the end of the text. If we do, there can be no more matches. We are not overrunning if the position pt added to the length of the word W is less than or equal to the length of the text T—that is, between these two positions:

```
          1         2
T 012345678901234567890123456789012345678
  houses and horses and hearses

W 012345
  horses

W                      012345
                       horses
```

That is, when pt is between 0 and 23 inclusive. So, we write this condition into our
program, using the **if**, **then**, and **length** keywords, as shown in the following listing.

Listing 4.2   Making sure we do not overrun the end

```
1 define search pt
2   if pt + length W <= length T then
3     ...
```

The <= symbol means "less than or equal to." Note that the dots . . . at line 3 are not
part of the program. They just show that we have not yet filled in what happens if our
condition is true. We have indented (moved to the right) line 2 by two spaces as well.
We use indentation to indicate structure in our program.

Now we need to fill in the rest of the search procedure, as shown in listing 4.3. We
want to perform the comparison of the word with the text at the current position, and
if it matches, we want to print out the position on the screen.

Listing 4.3   Checking for a match

```
1 define search pt
2   if pt + length W <= length T then
3     if compare pt 0 then print pt
```

Here, we are using the yet-to-be-concocted compare algorithm to compare the text W
with the text T at position pt. It has another parameter, which it will use as a counter. We
start the counter at 0. We don't need to know how compare works yet, just what it does
with what it is given. This convenient blindness is what allows us to construct programs
piece by piece in a modular fashion, replacing individual parts without changing the
rules that connect them. Now, whether or not we found a match, it is time to move on
to the next position: we run search again, adding 1 to the position pt, as shown in the
following listing.

Listing 4.4   Moving on

```
1 define search pt
2   if pt + length W <= length T then
3     if compare pt 0 then print pt
4     search (pt + 1)
```

Note that, due to the indentation, both lines 3 and 4 only happen if the `if` condition on line 2 is met. Now, see what happens when we execute our program on our example word horses and text horses and houses and hearses:

```
W = horses
T = houses and horses and hearses
```

search 0	search 9	search 17
search 1	search 10	search 18
search 2	search 11	search 19
search 3	11	search 20
search 4	search 12	search 21
search 5	search 13	search 22
search 6	search 14	search 23
search 7	search 15	
search 8	search 16	

Here, we have shown not only the matching position that our program prints but also a summary of the execution of our program to help us to understand what is going on. A match is found at position 11, as required, and the program stops after position 23. At least for this example, our program seems to work. Run through it on paper yourself to check. Now, we must fill in the gap: we have pretended that compare already exists. In reality, we need to write such an algorithm. We begin by defining it, just like for search, as shown in the following listing.

Listing 4.5   Beginning our comparison function

```
1 define compare pt pw
```

The compare function will differ from the search function in an important way: the search function prints things to the screen, whereas the compare algorithm will calculate one of two special values: either `true` or `false`. This information will be passed back to the search function so it can decide what to do. The compare function has two parameters: pt, the same one as search, and one more, pw, which is the position in the word.

We will first compare position pt in the text T with position pw in the word W and then pt + 1 with pw + 1, etc. Remember that when we wrote search, we started pw at 0 when using compare. As soon as we find a mismatch, we stop and return `false`. If we reach the end of the word without finding such a mismatch, we stop and return `true` because the whole word must have matched. We dispense with the success condition first: if pw is equal to length pw, it means we have successfully compared positions 0 to pw - 1, and so we can return `true`, as shown in the following listing.

Listing 4.6   Checking whether we have finished

```
1 define compare pt pw
2   if pw = length W then return true
```

Now, we must test the character at position pt in T and the character at position pw in W to see whether they are equal, as shown in listing 4.7. We access the individual characters by writing, for example, W[pw], where W is the word and pw is the position.

Listing 4.7 Checking one character

```
1 define compare pt pw
2   if pw = length W then return true
3   if T[pt] = W[pw] then compare (pt + 1) (pw + 1)
```

If the two characters are equal, we continue by running compare with both the text and word positions advanced by 1. All that remains now is to return false if they were not equal, as shown in the following listing.

Listing 4.8 The failure case

```
1 define compare pt pw
2   if pw = length W then return true
3   if T[pt] = W[pw] then compare (pt + 1) (pw + 1)
4   return false
```

This line will only be reached if the condition at line 3 was false. The following listing provides the whole program in one place.

Listing 4.9 The whole program

```
1 define compare pt pw
2   if pw = length W then return true
3   if T[pt] = W[pw] then compare (pt + 1) (pw + 1)
4   return false
5
6 define search pt
7   if pt + length W <= length T then
8     if compare pt 0 then print pt
9     search (pt + 1)
```

Our made-up language is not so dissimilar to some real computer languages. Some of the words are different, but the essential features are there. Let's take a more detailed look at the execution of our search by giving a running commentary of the parameters given to search and compare in figure 4.1.

We can see in the figure that, most of the time, compare fails on the first letter in the word, and we do not need to proceed further. When a match is found, every letter must be checked, of course. At positions 0 and 22, we have to check more than the first letter to see that there is no match. You can run the whole thing through on paper if you like.

```
W = horses
T = houses and horses and hearses
```

```
search 0             search 9            compare 15 0
compare 0 0          compare 9 0         search 16
compare 1 1          search 10           compare 16 0
search 1             compare 10 0        search 17
compare 1 0          search 11           compare 17 0
search 2             compare 11 0        search 18
compare 2 0          compare 11 1        compare 18 0
search 3             compare 11 2        search 19
compare 3 0          compare 11 3        compare 19 0
search 4             compare 11 4        search 20
compare 4 0          compare 11 5        compare 20 0
search 5             11                  search 21
compare 5 0          search 12           compare 21 0
search 6             compare 12 0        search 22
compare 6 0          search 13           compare 22 0
search 7             compare 13 0        compare 22 1
compare 7 0          search 14           search 23
search 8             compare 14 0        compare 23 0
compare 8 0          search 15
```

Figure 4.1   Each use of `search` and `compare`

4.3   Speed

How much work did we have to do to find out whether there was a match? Let's consider comparing two letters as our basic unit of work: How many times did we have to do it? Consider figure 4.2. We make a total of 32 comparisons. (The number of comparisons is written at the right on each line.) We make sure that our compare function fails as soon as possible but make no other efficiencies. We are lucky that h does not appear in English very often; if our search word began with e, we would have to make many more second-letter comparisons. Let's call the length of the word l_W and the length of the text l_T and find the minimum and maximum number of comparisons in general. In the best case, the word never matches on the first letter, so we always have one comparison each time. The total, then, is just $l_T - l_W + 1$. (We take away l_W because we stop when the word overruns the end of the text.) In our example, that is $29 - 6 + 1 = 24$ (for example, searching for

```
                       1         2
T 012345678901234567890123456789012345678
  houses and horses and hearses

W 012345
  horses   3
   horses   1
    horses   1
     horses   1
      horses   1
       horses   1
        horses   1
         horses   1
          horses   1
           horses   1
            horses   1
             horses   6
              horses   1
               horses   1
                horses   1
                 horses   1
                  horses   1
                   horses   1
                    horses   1
                     horses   1
                      horses   1
                       horses   1
                        horses   1
                         horses   2
                          horses   1
```

Figure 4.2   Each comparison in our search

zebras since z will never match). In the worst case, we have to go all the way to the last character to see whether a match occurs (for example, searching for aaaaab in aaaaaaaaaaaaaaaaaaaaaaaaaaaaa). Then we need six comparisons for each position, which, in general, is $l_W \times (l_T - l_W + 1)$ or, in our case, $6 \times (29 - 6 + 1) = 6 \times 24 = 144$. Calculations such as these are vital in computer science. We must know how our algorithm performs as the size of the problem increases. This algorithm performs reasonably well: if the text size doubles, it takes twice as long, just as we might expect.

We have now written out our basic algorithm and shown how to calculate how long it takes. As you may have guessed, the total time taken to run this algorithm on our toy example is essentially zero. However, computers often need to search through enormous amounts of data, and improving our algorithm can make a huge difference in these cases. We will now discuss an improvement to our rather naive searching algorithm, making it more practical for use on larger pieces of data—imagine searching through your whole computer's storage for a word or phrase, for example.

4.4 A faster algorithm

The field of searching algorithms is vast and complex, but we will consider one of the simpler improvements: skipping forward more than one place when we know for some reason that a match cannot now happen. For example, let's consider the first position again:

```
          1         2
T 012345678901234567890123456789
  houses and horses and hearses

W 012345
  horses
```

The h matches, and then the o, but the r in the word does not match the u in the text. Since there is no u anywhere in horses, we can skip ahead to position 3 immediately:

```
          1         2
T 012345678901234567890123456789
  houses and horses and hearses

W 012345
  horses   3
     horses
```

Let's apply such skipping rules to our whole search and see how many comparisons are now required. Look at figure 4.3.

We skipped two times. The first time as described already: there is no u in the word horses. The second time was when we found a match: since there is no h anywhere else in horses, we may skip six places. Therefore, we reduce the number of comparisons from 32 to 23.

We have produced a very simple searching method and shown how it works. In reality, things are more complex. How do we deal with case (`Horses` vs. `horses`), different parts of speech (`horsed around with`), accents (`cafe` and `café`), ligatures (`haemoglobin` and `hæmoglobin`), and so forth?

Of course, even with our existing search program, we can search for things other than words, such as `!!` to look for excessive punctuation, or `and and` to search for a common mistake. So let's stop calling the thing we search for a *word* and instead call it a *pattern*. The simplest examples of patterns are what we have been using already: they find only a piece of the text that matches the pattern exactly. More advanced patterns consist of special characters to indicate a loosening of the requirements for one or more characters to match. For example, we can write `realise|realize` to search for either `realise` or `realize`. (You can find the `|` symbol on your computer keyboard if you look carefully. In this context, we pronounce it *or* because it looks for the thing on its left or the thing on its right, matching in either case.) In fact, we can simplify this pattern by using parentheses to limit the optional section and write `reali(s|z)e`. This will still match `realize` and `realise`. There are other special characters: for example, we can use a full stop `.` to match any character, so the pattern `.unce` matches `ounce` and `dunce`.

In addition to these patterns, we can run a search multiple times and combine the results. For example, when using an internet search engine, if we are interested in finding documents containing `cats` or `dogs`, we might enter the search `cats OR dogs`. The search engine knows that the word `OR` is special and runs two searches, one for `cats` and one for `dogs`, and returns documents that contain an instance of either. In reality, search engines don't look through the text of web pages at the moment you click the search button: they use pre-prepared indexes to make the search many, many times faster.

In the problems that follow, this idea of patterns is extended and you are asked to run the searching algorithm through on paper to determine whether they match the text.

```
                1                   2
T  012345678901234567890123456789012345678
   houses and horses and hearses

W  012345
   horses   3
      horses   1
       horses   1
        horses   1
         horses   1
          horses   1
           horses   1
            horses   1
             horses   1
              horses   6
                  horses   1
                   horses   1
                    horses   1
                     horses   1
                      horses   1
                       horses   2
```

Figure 4.3   Skipping unneeded comparisons

Problems

For solutions, see appendix B.

1 Run the `search` procedure against the following patterns and this text:

```
The source of sorrow is the self itself
```

What happens each time?

(a) `cow`

(b) `row`

(c) `self`

(d) `the`

2 Consider the following kind of advanced pattern syntax and give example texts that match the following patterns. A question mark ? indicates that zero or one of the previous letters is to be matched; an asterisk * indicates zero or more; a plus sign + indicates one or more. Parentheses around two letters separated by a | allow either letter to occur. The letters ?, +, and * may follow such a closing parenthesis with the effect of operating on whichever letter is chosen.

(a) `aa+`

(b) `ab?c`

(c) `ab*c`

(d) `a(b|c)*d`

3 Assuming we have a version of `search` that works for these advanced patterns, give the results of running it on the same text as in problem 1.

(a) `r+ow`

(b) `(T|t)he`

(c) `(T|t)?he`

(d) `(T|t)*he`

Summary

- Computer programs for a real-world task, such as searching in text, are built step by reasoned step. Every function of your computer is built like this.
- We can test our program by going through its operation manually on paper.
- Computers run many hundreds of millions of such little algorithms each second, hard though it is for us to comprehend.
- Due to the huge size of the data our programs may need to work with, attention to efficiency is second only in importance to attention to correctness when programming.

Typing it in

This chapter covers

- The development of the keyboard and typewriter
- Modern input methods for the computer
- Typing languages such as Chinese

It is easy to take for granted the ability to enter, modify, and correct large amounts of text accurately and quickly since most of us have some proficiency in it these days. But remember that, in the past, huge numbers of young people would go to secretarial school before they could work as typists or data entry clerks. The present generation may use computer or tablet keyboards from childhood, but those of us who remember having to learn to type as teenagers recall how hard it seemed at the time. In this chapter, we will look at different keyboard configurations, including those that can accommodate languages other than English.

5.1 Beginnings

The development of the keyboard began before the computer, of course, for typewriters and similar equipment. And so, when computers were first developed, the best methods for text input were already known, requiring only slight alteration. In this chapter, we will look at the development of typing devices from the typewriter to the modern computer. We will also see methods for typing languages such as Chinese, where the number of characters might vastly outnumber the keys that can possibly be placed on a keyboard.

As early as the 18th century, work was beginning on devices for "automatic writing," but what we recognize today as a typewriter can be traced back to the first commercially successful examples, the work of the Pennsylvania-born newspaper editor Christopher Latham Sholes (1819–1890). His company was eventually sold to Remington & Sons, under whose brand typewriters were sold until the 1960s.

Figure 5.1 shows the Type Writing Machine of C.L. Sholes, 1868. It is unrecognizable as a modern typewriter, with piano-style keys and the paper held horizontally. Only a few units were produced commercially before money ran out. Development of a new, more practical design continued. An early user of a demonstration machine, James Densmore, bought a 25% interest in the project, despite believing that it needed significant further development to be practical.

Figure 5.2 shows Sholes's improved Type Writing Machine of 1878. This machine is rather more recognizable as a typewriter to modern eyes, with four rows of keys in roughly the same arrangement as computer keyboards today and the paper clipped into a rotating drum, allowing for secure and reliable placement of each row. There is a foot pedal for advancing to the next line. You can see the key arrangement here. Note that there are no keys for 0 (zero) or 1 (one) since the keys for O (capital o) and I (capital i) were deemed similar enough. The machines were already complex, unreliable, and difficult and expensive to manufacture; anything that could reduce complexity was welcome.

5.2 Layouts

Figure 5.3 shows the arrangement of piano-style keys on Sholes's first typewriter. You can see that the alphabetic characters are largely in order. This arrangement caused mechanical problems with the machine. When a key was pressed, a *type-bar* with the correct letter would swing up to hit the paper. It would then fall back down by gravity. However, once a user became proficient and was hitting keys one after another in quick succession, the falling type-bar could rub against the next rising one, jamming, especially if the keys were next to one another in the row of type-bars.

The keyboard was redesigned by analyzing the English language to determine which letters commonly followed one another and moving them apart on the keyboard. This development led to the QWERTY arrangement, which is almost ubiquitous today. It also led to the urban myth that the QWERTY keyboard was intended to "slow the typist down because the machine could not cope." In fact, the rearrangement facilitated *faster* typing. Figure 5.4 shows the keyboard layout from one of Sholes's later patents.

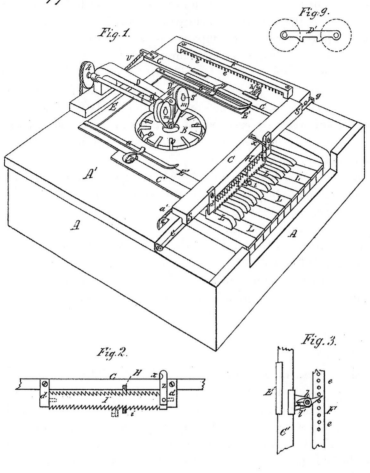

Figure 5.1   **The Type Writing Machine of C.L. Sholes, 1868 (front view)**

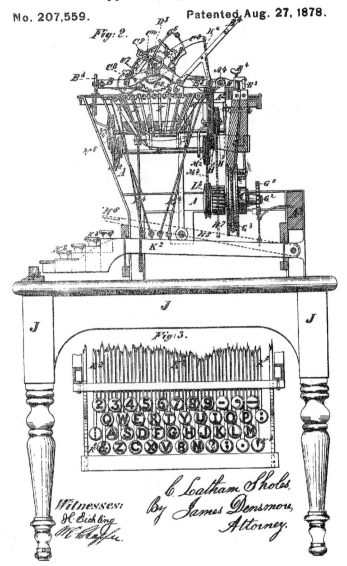

Figure 5.2   The Type Writing Machine of C.L. Sholes, 1878 (side view and keyboard)

Figure 5.3   The arrangement of keys on the early Sholes keyboard

The most common (although still rather uncommon) alternative keyboard layout is the *Dvorak* layout, patented in 1936 by August Dvorak (1894–1975), a professor at the University of Washington. His layout, as specified in his patent, is shown in figure 5.5. The layout has

Figure 5.4   Keys arranged for faster typing

been modified slightly over the years by Dvorak and the American National Standards Institute. The intent was to design, by scientific methods, a keyboard layout that is optimal for the typist, irrespective of the demands of the machine being typed on. (We don't have to worry about jamming type-bars in the computer age.) The layout places the most common keys in the middle row, under the hands, and the least common, on the bottom row where it is most awkward to reach. The keys are arranged left and right so that, commonly, keypresses alternate between the left and right hands in a rhythmic fashion. The layout has never caught on, however, although one can buy keyboards for most modern computers with the Dvorak layout, and it retains a band of admirers.

It is striking how similar the keyboards of these early typewriters are to those we use every day. Figure 5.6 shows a keyboard from the early days of computing. It belongs to the UNIVAC system built by the Eckert-Mauchly Computer Corporation in 1953.

By the 1980s, computer keyboards were almost identical in layout to today's, just rather larger and more solid. Figure 5.7 is an IBM Model M Keyboard from 1985.

My own keyboard (Apple, 2015), with which this book was typed, is much the same but very much thinner and lighter. It is shown in figure 5.8. Laptop keyboards must be smaller and thinner still.

5.3   *Other languages*

What of languages other than English? We can divide them into three categories. First, some keyboards use the *Latin* alphabet (that is, the familiar ABC) but contain characters with accents or one or two extra characters only. Typically, these characters can be typed on a standard keyboard, using either modifier keys (holding down a key to make the next letter accented) or by using short sequences of keys (typing "`" followed by the "a" key for "à"). The second category is those languages, such as Modern Greek or Russian, that do not use the Latin alphabet but whose alphabet has only a few 10s of characters. These can be dealt with by using the same keyboard, simply with different letters printed on it. The last category is for languages such as Chinese. There are many tens of thousands of characters, and it is impractical to build or use a keyboard with that many keys. Some system must be devised to allow all these characters to be typed on a limited number of keys. This approach is known as an *input system*.

One such input system in use in China, Singapore, and Taiwan is *Pinyin*. It requires knowing the pronunciation of the word: Westernized spellings of the syllables are then used to find the right character. We can write the word 櫻桃, which means cherry. In

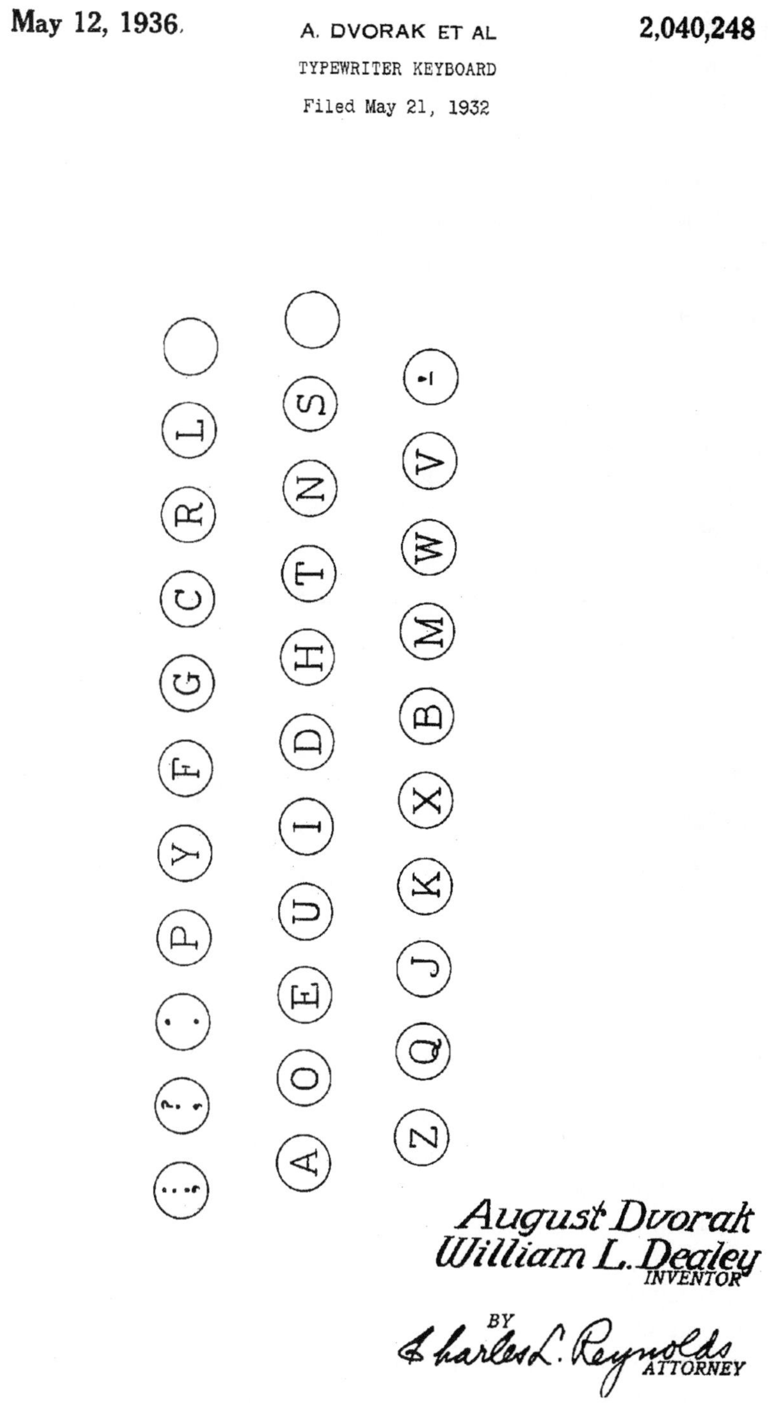

May 12, 1936.

A. DVORAK ET AL   2,040,248

TYPEWRITER KEYBOARD

Filed May 21, 1932

August Dvorak
William L. Dealey
INVENTOR

BY

Charles L. Reynolds
ATTORNEY

Figure 5.5   The Dvorak keyboard layout

Figure 5.6   The UNIVAC keyboard. (Photo courtesy of the Retrocomputing Society of Rhode Island)

Figure 5.7   The IBM Model M keyboard. (Photo courtesy of Sal Cangeloso)

Figure 5.8   A modern Apple keyboard

the Pinyin system, we type the Western characters representing the sounds, and we are then invited to disambiguate among the possibilities as the word is formed.

The word for cherry sounds like "ying" followed by "tao." First, we type "ying," as shown in figure 5.9. The computer displays a list of possibilities for the first character of our word. It does not yet know which syllable or syllables may follow. We choose the right one, and the computer replaces "ying" with the proper character, as shown in figure 5.10. Now, we type the second syllable "tao". We are again invited to choose a character from a list. We choose the correct one by clicking or typing a number, and the word is complete, as shown in figure 5.11.

Another input method for Chinese is *Zhuyin*. This system uses about 40 basic characters, which can be arranged on a normal computer keyboard, as shown in figure 5.12. The symbols are on the top right of each key. These characters can be used to represent all

Figure 5.9 Beginning our word

Figure 5.10 Choosing the right character

Figure 5.11 Finishing our word

Figure 5.12 A Zhuyin keyboard

sounds in the language. Just like in Pinyin, the sounds lead to the characters. However, unlike Pinyin, there is no need for the user to know any Western characters at all.

Let's type 櫻桃 using the Zhuyin system. We begin by typing one of the characters that represent sounds, as shown in figure 5.13. We continue to build the first character by typing the next Zhuyin symbol, as shown in figure 5.14. Now, we type in the *tone* using the number keys on the keyboard, as shown in figure 5.15 (there are four tones in Chinese, each a different variation on a given sound). We can now see the full character, which replaces the Zhuyin ones we typed in. It is the wrong character, but do not worry:

Figure 5.13 Typing the first sound character

Figure 5.14 Adding the next Zhuyin symbol

it will correct itself once the system knows the end of the word. We begin on the second character, as shown in figure 5.16.

Figure 5.15   **Using the number keys to indicate tone**

Figure 5.16   **Beginning the second character**

Now we type the second sound of the second character, as shown in figure 5.17. Again, we choose the tone. Contextual information, such as the previous character, is used to disambiguate the two-character sequence, and in this case, the most common possibility is correct, as shown in figure 5.18.

Figure 5.17   **The next Zhuyin symbol for our second character**

Figure 5.18   **The word is finished.**

Different systems are popular in each part of Asia and in each generation and depend upon the device in use. Indeed, one person may use a particular system on their computer and entirely another on their mobile phone, which has even less space for keys (real or virtual).

In this chapter, we have seen how English and the world's many other languages might be typed into the computer. There have been many attempts to replace the keyboard for text input, such as voice recognition, which have made some inroads in automotive and niche applications. However, for general-purpose computing, the keyboard, real or virtual, still reigns.

Summary

- The modern computer keyboard has an almost 150-year history, the vestiges of which are still apparent today.
- Languages using the Latin alphabet can be handled by using modifier keys for accents or with short sequences of keys on a standard keyboard.
- Languages that do not use the Latin alphabet (for example, Modern Greek) can be handled with the same keyboard, but with different letters printed on it.

- Non-Western languages, such as Chinese, that are built from a multitude of characters require more complicated input methods, such as specialized keyboards or onscreen character comparison lists.
- Even devices without physical keyboards, like smartphones, often use a screen-based version of a keyboard.

Saving space 6

This chapter covers

- Reducing the size of data by compression
- Simple compression of text by substitution
- Advanced compression with frequency counts

As computers get ever faster, we ask ever more of them: a high-resolution film streamed in real time, a faster download, or the same experience on a mobile device over a slow connection as we have at home or in the office over a fast one. When we talk of efficiency, we are concerned with the time taken to do a task, the space required to store data, and secondary effects such as how often we have to charge our device's battery. And so we cannot simply say, "Things are getting faster all the time; we need not worry about efficiency." In this chapter, we will delve into one tool for managing the size of information: compression.

6.1 Compression

An important tool for reducing the space information takes up (and so increasing the speed with which it can be moved around) is *compression*. The idea is to process the information in such a way that it not only becomes smaller but also so that it may be *decompressed*. In other words, the process must be reversible.

Imagine we want to send a coffee order. Instead of writing "Four espressos, two double espressos, a cappuccino, and two lattes," we might write "4E2DC2L." This format relies, of course, on the person to whom we are sending the order knowing how to decompress it. The instructions for decompressing might be longer than the message itself, but if we are sending similar messages each day, we need only share the instructions once. We have reduced the message from 67 characters to 7, making it almost 10 times smaller.

This sort of compression happens routinely, and it is really just a matter of choosing a better representation for storing a particular kind of information. It tends to be more successful the more uniform the data is. Can we come up with a compression method that works for any data? If not, what about one that works well for a whole class of data, such as text in the English language, photographs, or video?

First, we should address the question of whether this kind of universal compression is even possible. Imagine that our message is just one character long, and our alphabet (our set of possible characters) is the familiar A,B,C . . . z. There are then exactly 26 different possible messages, each consisting of a single character. Assuming each message is equally likely, there is no way to reduce the length of messages and thus compress them. In fact, this is not entirely true: we can make a tiny improvement: we can send the empty message for, say, A, and then 1 out of 26 messages would be smaller. What about a message of length two? Again, if all messages are equally likely, we can do no better: if we were to encode some of the two-letter sequences using just one letter, we would have to use two-letter sequences to indicate the one-letter ones and, therefore, would have gained nothing. The same argument applies to sequences of length three, four, or five or, indeed, of any length. However, all is not lost.

6.2   *Patterns*

Most information has patterns, or elements that are more or less common, in it. For example, most of the words in this book can be found in an English dictionary. When there are patterns, we can reserve our shorter codes for the most common sequences, reducing the overall length of the message. It is not immediately apparent how to go about this, so we will proceed by example. Consider the text in figure 6.1, from

Whether it was embarrassment or impatience, the judge rocked backwards and forwards on his seat. The man behind him, whom he had been talking with earlier, leant forward again, either to give him a few general words of encouragement or some specific piece of advice. Below them in the hall the people talked to each other quietly but animatedly. The two factions had earlier seemed to hold views strongly opposed to each other but now they began to intermingle, a few individuals pointed up at K., others pointed at the judge. The air in the room was fuggy and extremely oppressive, those who were standing furthest away could hardly even be seen through it. It must have been especially troublesome for those visitors who were in the gallery, as they were forced to quietly ask the participants in the assembly what exactly was happening, albeit with timid glances at the judge. The replies they received were just as quiet, and given behind the protection of a raised hand.

Figure 6.1   Our example text, from Metamorphosis by Franz Kafka

Metamorphosis by Franz Kafka. We will take as our dictionary the hundred-most commonly used English words of three or more letters, as shown in figure 6.2.

00	the	17	not	34	about	51	more	68	down	85	year
01	and	18	what	35	out	52	write	69	day	86	live
02	you	19	all	36	many	53	see	70	did	87	back
03	that	20	were	37	then	54	number	71	get	88	give
04	was	21	when	38	them	55	way	72	come	89	most
05	for	22	your	39	these	56	could	73	made	90	very
06	are	23	can	40	some	57	people	74	may	91	after
07	with	24	said	41	her	58	than	75	part	92	thing
08	his	25	there	42	would	59	first	76	over	93	our
09	they	26	use	43	make	60	water	77	new	94	just
10	this	27	each	44	like	61	been	78	sound	95	name
11	have	28	which	45	him	62	call	79	take	96	good
12	from	29	she	46	into	63	who	80	only	97	sentence
13	one	30	how	47	time	64	its	81	little	98	man
14	had	31	their	48	has	65	now	82	work	99	think
15	word	32	will	49	look	66	find	83	know		
16	but	33	other	50	two	67	long	84	place		

Figure 6.2   The 100 most-used English words of three or more letters

These words will be compressed by representing them as the two-character sequences 00, 01, 02, . . . , 97, 98, 99. We don't bother with the one- and two-letter words, common though they are, because they are already as short or shorter than our codes. We assume our text does not contain digits so that any digit sequence may be interpreted as a code. Any word, text, or punctuation not in the word list will be rendered literally. If we substitute these codes into our text, we find a somewhat underwhelming level of compression, as seen in figure 6.3.

Whether it 04 embarrassment or impatience, 00 judge rocked backwards 01 forwards on 08 seat. The 98 behind 45, whom he 14 61 talking 07 earlier, leant forward again, either to 88 45 a few general 15s of encouragement or 40 specific piece of advice. Below 38 in 00 hall 00 people talked to 27 33 quietly 16 animatedly. The 50 factions 14 earlier seemed to views strongly opposed to 27 33 16 65 09 began to intermingle, a few individuals pointed up to K., 33s pointed at 00 judge. The air in 00 room 04 fuggy 01 extremely oppressive, those 63 20 standing furthest away could hardly ever be 53n through it. It must 11 61 especially troublesome 05 those visitors 63 20 in 00 gallery, as 09 20 forced to quietly ask 00 participants in 00 assembly 18 exactly 04 happening, albeit 07 timid glances at 00 judge. The replies 09 received 20 94 as quiet, 01 given behind 00 protection of a raised hand.

Figure 6.3   Compression with common words

The original text had 975 characters; the new one has 891. One more small change can be made: where there is a sequence of codes, we can squash them together if they have only spaces between them in the source. This is shown in figure 6.4.

Whether it 04 embarrassment or impatience, 00 judge rocked backwards 01 forwards on 08 seat. The 98 behind 45, whom he 1461 talking 07 earlier, leant forward again, either to 8845 a few general 15s of encouragement or 40 specific piece of advice. Below 38 in 00 hall 00 people talked to 2733 quietly 16 animatedly. The 50 factions 14 earlier seemed to views strongly opposed to 2733166509 began to intermingle, a few individuals pointed up to K., 33s pointed at 00 judge. The air in 00 room 04 fuggy 01 extremely oppressive, those 6320 standing furthest away could hardly ever be 53n through it. It must 11 61 especially troublesome 05 those visitors 6320 in 00 gallery, as 0920 forced to quietly ask 00 participants in 00 assembly 18 exactly 04 happening, albeit 07 timid glances at 00 judge. The replies 09 received 2094 as quiet, 01 given behind 00 protection of a raised hand.

Figure 6.4   Squashing codes together

We are down to 880 characters, a reduction of about 10% compared to the original. The top 100 words in English are known to cover about half of the printed words, in general. We have not quite achieved that in this example.

6.3   *Frequency*

Let's try counting the number of each character in our text to see whether we can take advantage of the fact that some letters are more common than others (our current method makes no use of the fact that, for example, spaces are very common). Figure 6.5 shows the character counts for our example text.

167	space	55	i	42	n	24	w	19	c	13	b	5	k	2	x	1	B
120	e	51	h	41	s	19	p	18	u	10	v	4	j	1	W		
71	t	49	o	33	d	19	m	15	y	10	,	4	T	1	K		
62	a	45	r	30	l	19	g	13	f	8	.	3	q	1	I		

Figure 6.5   Character frequencies in our text

The space character is, by far, the most common (we say it has the highest frequency). The frequencies of the lowercase letters are roughly what we might expect from recalling the value of Scrabble tiles: the punctuation characters are infrequent, and the capital letters are very infrequent.

We have talked about what a bit is, how 8 bits make a byte, and how 1 byte is sufficient to store a character (at least in English). Our original message is 975 bytes, or $975 \times 8 = 7,800$ bits. We could encode each of the 33 characters we have found in our text using a different pattern of 6 bits, since 33 is less than 64, which is the number of 6-bit combinations $000000, 000001, \ldots, 111110, 111111$. (The number of 5-bit combinations is 32, which is not quite enough.) This approach would reduce our space to $975 \times 6 =$

5,850 bits. However, we would have wasted many of the possible sets of codes and taken no advantage of our knowledge of how frequently each character occurs.

What we want is a code that uses shorter bit patterns for more common characters and longer bit patterns for less common ones. The beginnings of such a code are shown in figure 6.6. There is a problem, though. Although we can easily encode a word—for example, *heat* encodes as 1110100 (that is, 11 for *h*, 1 for *e*, 01 for *a*, and 00 for *t*)—we can decode it in many different ways. The sequence 1110100 might equally be taken to mean "*eeespaceespace*" or "*hiispace*." Our code is ambiguous. What we require is a code with the so-called *prefix property*—that is, arranged such that no code in the table is a prefix of another. For example, we cannot have both 001 and 0010 as codes since 001 appears at the beginning of 0010. This property allows for unambiguous decoding. Consider the alternative code in figure 6.7.

space	0		space	00
e	1		e	010
t	00		t	011
a	01		a	100
i	10		i	101
h	11		h	110
o	000		o	111
⋮	⋮		⋮	⋮

Figure 6.6   A naive code with increasing bit length   **Figure 6.7   An unambiguous code**

This code is unambiguous: no code is a prefix of another. The word "heat" encodes as 110010100011 and may be decoded unambiguously. We can have the computer automatically create an appropriate code for our text, taking into account the frequencies. Then, by sending the code table along with the text, we ensure it can be unambiguously decoded. Figure 6.8 shows the full table of unambiguous codes for the frequencies derived from our text.

space	111	o	0011	w	00011	y	010111	k	11000011	K	010110000
e	100	r	0010	p	110101	f	010101	j	11000001	l	1100001011
t	1011	n	0000	m	110100	b	010100	T	11000000	B	1100001010
a	0111	s	11011	g	110011	v	000101	q	01011001		
i	0110	d	10101	c	110010	,	000100	x	110000100		
h	0100	l	10100	u	110001	.	0101101	W	010110001		

Figure 6.8   Full code for our text

The information in this table can, alternatively, be viewed as a diagram, as shown in figure 6.9.

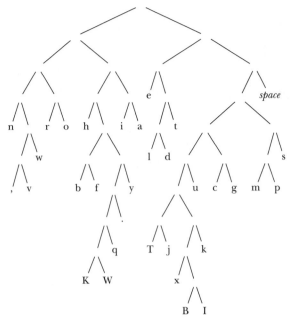

Figure 6.9   Our code table as a tree

To find the code for a letter, we start at the top, adding 0 each time we go left and 1 each time we go right. For example, the code for the letter "g" is Right Right Left Left Right Right or 110011. All the letters are at the bottom edge of the diagram, a visual reinforcement of the prefix property. The compressed message length for our example text is 4,171 bits or 522 bytes, about half of the original message length. Sending the tree requires another 197 bits or 25 bytes. (The method is not discussed here.) Of course, the longer the message, the less it matters since the message will be so big by comparison. These codes are called *Huffman codes* after David A. Huffman, who invented them while a PhD student at MIT in the 1950s.

6.4   *Compressing images*

A common use for this sort of encoding is in the sending of faxes. (Younger readers may need reminding that faxes were a pre-internet method of sending pictures over an ordinary telephone line with the machine at the sending end scanning a piece of paper as the machine at the receiving end printed to another.) A fax consists of a high-resolution black-and-white image. In this case, we are not compressing characters but the black-and-white image of those characters itself. Take the fragment shown in figure 6.10. This image is 37 pixels wide and 15 pixels tall. Figure 6.11 shows it with a grid superimposed to make it easier to count pixels.

We cannot compress the whole thing with Huffman encoding since we do not know the frequencies at the outset given that a fax is sent incrementally. One machine scans the document while the machine at the other end of the phone line prints the result

Figure 6.10   A fragment of a fax image

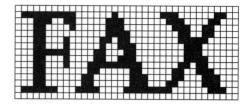

Figure 6.11   A fragment of a fax image with boxes for pixels

as it pulls paper from its roll. It had to be this way because when fax machines were in their infancy, computer memory was very expensive, so receiving and storing the whole image in one go and only then printing it out was not practical.

The solution the fax system uses is as follows. Instead of sending individual pixels, a fax sends a list of *runs* a line at a time. Each run is a length of white pixels or a length of black pixels. For example, a line of width 39 might contain 12 pixels of white, then 4 of black, then 2 of white, then 18 of black, and then 3 of white. We look up the code for each run and send the codes in order. To avoid the problem of having to gather frequency data for the whole page, a pre-prepared master code table is used, upon which everyone agrees. The table has been built by gathering frequencies from thousands of text documents in several languages and typefaces and then collating the frequencies of the various black-and-white runs.

Figure 6.12 is the table of codes for black-and-white runs of lengths 0 to 63. (We need length 0 because a line is always assumed to begin white, and a zero-length white run is required if the line actually begins black.)

Notice that the prefix property applies only to alternating black-and-white codes. There is never a black code followed by a black code or a white code followed by a white code. The shortest codes are reserved for the most common runs: the black ones of length two and three. We can write out the codes for the first two lines of our image by counting the pixels manually, as shown in figure 6.13.

So we transmit the bit pattern 00010110 0000111 000100 1110 010 1111 10 1110 0111. The number of bits required to transmit the image has dropped from $37 \times 2 = 74$ to $8 + 7 + 6 + 4 + 3 + 4 + 2 + 4 + 2 + 4 = 46$. Due to the preponderance of white space in written text (blank lines, spaces between words, and page margins), faxes can often be compressed to less than 20% of their original size. Modern fax systems, which take advantage of the fact that successive lines are often similar, can reduce this to 5%.

6.5   *Shades of gray*

Of course, we often want more than just black and white. (Even black-and-white television was not really just black and white; there were shades of gray.) How can we compress gray and color photographic images? The reversible (lossless) compression we have used so far tends not to work well, so we must look at methods that do not retain all the information in an image. This is known as *lossy compression*. One option is simply to use

Run	White	Black	Run	White	Black
0	00110101	0000110111	32	00011011	000001101010
1	0000111	010	33	00010010	000001101011
2	0111	11	34	00010011	000011010010
3	1000	10	35	00010100	000011010011
4	1011	011	36	00010101	000011010100
5	1100	0011	37	00010110	000011010101
6	1110	0010	38	00010111	000011010110
7	1111	00011	39	00101000	000011010111
8	1011	000101	40	00101001	000001101100
9	10100	000100	41	00101010	000001101101
10	00111	0000100	42	00101011	000011011010
11	01000	0000101	43	00101100	000011011011
12	001000	0000111	44	00101101	000001010100
13	000011	00000100	45	00000100	000001010101
14	110100	00000111	46	00000101	000001010110
15	110101	000011000	47	00001010	000001010111
16	101010	0000010111	48	0000101	00001100100
17	101011	0000011000	49	01010010	000001100101
18	0100111	0000001000	50	01010011	000001010010
19	0001100	00001100111	51	01010100	000001010011
20	0001000	00001101000	52	01010101	000000100100
21	0010111	00001101100	53	00100100	000000110111
22	00000011	00000110111	54	00100101	000000111000
23	0000100	00000101000	55	01011000	000000100111
24	0101000	00000010111	56	01011001	000000101000
25	0101011	00000011000	57	01011010	000001011000
26	0010011	000011001010	58	01011011	000001011001
27	0100100	000011001011	59	01001010	000000101011
28	0011000	000011001100	60	00110010	000000101100
29	00000010	000011001101	61	00110010	000001011010
30	00000011	000001101000	62	00110011	000001100110
31	00011010	000001101001	63	00110100	000001100111

Figure 6.12   Codes for black-and-white runs

fewer colors. Figure 6.14 shows a picture reduced from the original to 64, then 8, and then 2 grays. We see a marked decrease in size, but the quality declines rapidly. On the printed page, we can certainly see that 8 and 2 grays are too few, but 64 seems alright. On a computer screen, you would see that even 64 is a noticeable decrease in quality.

Run length	Color	Bit pattern	Pattern length
37	white	00010110	8
1	white	0000111	7
9	black	000100	6
6	white	1110	4
1	black	010	3
7	white	1111	4
3	black	10	2
6	white	1110	4
2	white	0111	4

Figure 6.13   Codes for the first two lines of our image

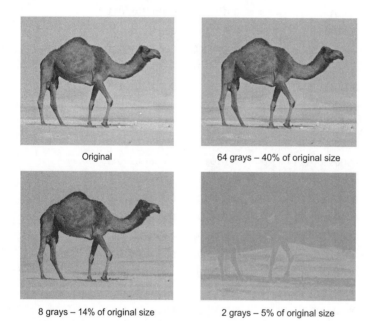

Original

64 grays – 40% of original size

8 grays – 14% of original size

2 grays – 5% of original size

Figure 6.14   Number of grays

If we can't reduce the number of grays with a satisfactory result, what about the resolution? Let's try discarding 1 out of every 2 pixels in each row of the original and 1 out of every 2 pixels in each column. Then, we will go further and discard 3 from every 4 and, finally, 7 from every 8. The result is figure 6.15. In these examples, we removed some information and then scaled up the image again when printing it on the page. Again, the first reduction is not too bad—at least at the printed size of this book. The 3/4 reduction is a little obvious, and the 7/8 reduction is dreadful. Algorithms have been devised that can take the images that have had data discarded like those in Figure 6.14 and, when scaling them back to normal size, attempt to smooth the image. This process reduces the "blocky" look, but it can lead to indistinctness. Figure 6.16 shows the same images as figure 6.15, displayed using a modern smoothing method.

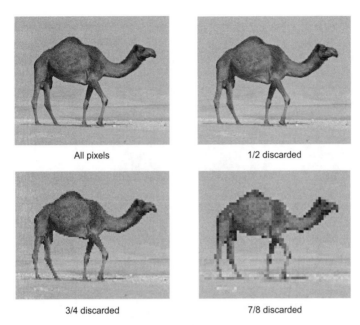

All pixels   1/2 discarded

3/4 discarded   7/8 discarded

Figure 6.15   Discarding rows of pixels

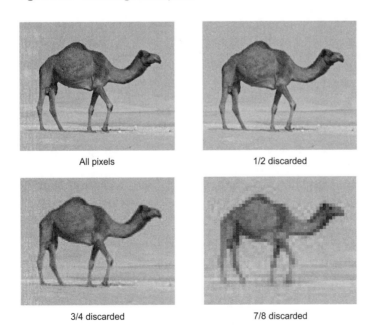

All pixels   1/2 discarded

3/4 discarded   7/8 discarded

Figure 6.16   Lower-resolution images displayed with smoothing

Finally, figure 6.17 shows the images compressed using a lossy compression algorithm especially intended for photographic use, the JPEG (Joint Photographic Experts Group) algorithm, first conceived in the 1980s. At 75% quality, the image is down to 19% of its original size and almost indistinguishable from the original.

The JPEG compression algorithm relies upon identifying parts of the image with little variation (for example, the sky and ground in our picture) and using less data to store approximations of them. The more detailed parts of the image, such as the camel itself, are stored in more detail. At higher-quality ratings, the eye should not be able to discern a difference.

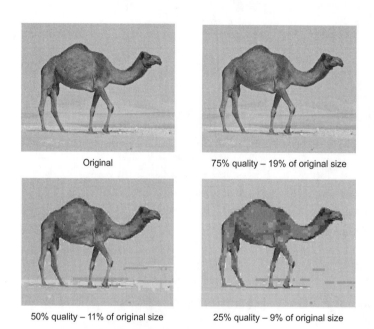

Original

75% quality – 19% of original size

50% quality – 11% of original size

25% quality – 9% of original size

Figure 6.17   JPEG compression

Problems

For solutions, see appendix B.

1 Count the frequencies of the characters in this piece of text from John Le Carré's *Tinker Tailor Soldier Spy* and assign them to the Huffman codes, filling in the following table. Then, encode the text up to "more lightly."

> "I have a theory which I suspect is rather immoral," Smiley went on, more lightly. "Each of us has only a quantum of compassion. That if we lavish our concern on every stray cat, we never get to the centre of things."

Letter	Frequency	Code	Letter	Frequency	Code
		111			110100
		100			110011
		1011			110010
		0111			110001
		0110			010111
		0100			010101
		0011			01010000
		0010			01010001
		0000			01010010
		11011			01010011
		10101			01011000
		10100			01011001
		00011			01011010
		110101			01011011

2 Consider the following frequency table and text. Decode it.

Letter	Frequency	Code	Letter	Frequency	Code
space	20	111	s	2	00011
e	12	100	d	2	110101
t	9	1011	T	1	110100
h	7	0111	n	1	110011
o	7	0110	w	1	110010
m	6	0100	p	1	110001
r	5	0011	b	1	010111
a	4	0010	l	1	010101
f	4	0000	v	1	01010000
c	4	11011	y	1	01010001
u	4	10101	.	1	01010010
i	3	10100			

```
110100011110000111001110010001110011101000110010010011001101100011111110010011110100110110111111001000111001110100000101101011001111010111000111101100000011101101100110111010010101011011011111100011011101010000000011100000110001111101101111000100111011010100000000111000001100011111011011110001001110110111010101110001010110100001010000100110101110010101111101101011100111101110100010010011110110111100010100011110110110111101110101001101010010
```

3 Encode the following fax image. There is no need to use zero-length white runs at the beginning of lines starting with a black pixel.

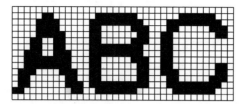

4 Decode the following fax image to the same 37×15 grid. There are no zero-length white runs at the beginning of lines starting with a black pixel.

```
000101100000011100011111100011110000011100000001001
011000010010000001000111111100101000101100100111
11100100000111111101101110111111101111111111011000
011111110010011111101111101111111100100000111000100
100011101111011100010001110001001000111011110111110
0010001111110010011111101011110111111100100000011111
1111011011111101111011111111011000011111111011011
11011101001111111011000011111111011011101111011110011
10001111101100001110000100100000001001000000010001
11000011100011111100101110001010110001011
```

Summary

- Computer information such as text, images, and especially video can have huge storage requirements and be slow to transmit from one place to another, even with today's technology.
- Compression is a vital mechanism to reduce these delays. It exploits patterns within the text or image to reduce its size.
- There are specialized compression methods for text and for still and video images.
- Compression may be lossless and, therefore, reversible, or lossy, throwing away carefully chosen information to reduce size further.

The sums behind the screen

7

This chapter covers

- How computers perform arithmetic
- Building larger programs from small parts
- Processing computer data such as lists

Almost everything discussed in this book—images, typefaces, encoding, laying out paragraphs—involves computer arithmetic in some form. In this chapter, we take a step back and try to answer a more fundamental question: How do computers calculate and programmers program? In this chapter, we'll look at the mathematics behind simple calculations, including arithmetic operations, functions, and data structures such as lists.

7.1 Simple calculations

How do we calculate the answer to $1 + 2 \times 3$? In our heads perhaps or on paper. But how do we decide which operation to do first (the + or the $\times$)? Well, in mathematics, we have the convention that, in this situation, the multiplication goes first. So we may work as follows:

$$1 + \underline{2 \times 3}$$
$$\implies \quad \underline{1 + 6}$$
$$\implies \quad 7$$

Something like $1 + 2 \times 3$ is an example of a mathematical *expression*. (We have underlined the part of the expression being worked on at each stage.) Rewriting it stage by stage, making it smaller each time until we reach a final answer, is called *evaluating* the expression. The result is a *value*, which is an expression that can be reduced no further: 7 is just 7. We could rewrite it as $3 + 4$ or $1 + 1 + 5$, of course, but we like each subsequent expression to be simpler than the last. Computer programs often involve these kinds of expressions, and indeed in some programming languages, the whole program is just one big expression.

It would be simpler if we could represent such expressions in an unambiguous way so that we don't need to think about the rules for which operations happen in which order. (It's simple in our example, but expressions in computer programs can be huge.) We can just add parentheses to the expression: $1 + (2 \times 3)$. Now the rule for choosing what to do next can be stated more simply: evaluate a part of the expression that contains no parentheses first. Note that for this to work, we have to parenthesize even expressions where the parentheses cannot affect the result—for example, $1 + (2 + (3 + 4))$.

It can be difficult for humans to read such overparenthesized expressions, which is why mathematicians use the minimum number of parentheses and rely on a set of ad hoc rules for disambiguation. The insistence on explicit preciseness can actually be antithetical to doing mathematics. For computers, however, this representation is ideal. We can see the structure of these expressions more clearly by drawing them like this:

is the same as $1 + (2 \times 3)$

These are called *trees* because they have a branching structure. Unlike real trees, we draw them upside down, with the *root* at the top. We can show the steps of evaluation just as before, without the need for any parentheses:

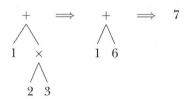

In fact, a computer would use this representation internally (not literal drawings, of course, but a structure of this form in its memory). When we type in a computer program using the keyboard, we might write `1 + 2 * 3`. (There is no × key on the keyboard.) It will be converted into tree form and can then be evaluated automatically and quickly by the computer.

7.2 *More general computation*

When we write instructions for computers, we want a single set of instructions to work for any given input. To do this, we write our expressions, just like in math, to use quantities like x and y and so on. These quantities are not fixed but can be different each time. We call them *variables*. For example, here is an expression that calculates the cube of a given number x:

When we evaluate this in an environment in which $x = 4$, we get one result:

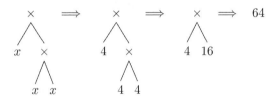

When we evaluate it instead in an environment in which $x = 50$, we get another:

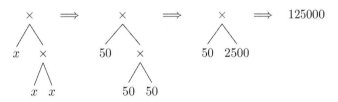

Of course, we can write the same thing out on a single line and evaluate it without drawing the tree explicitly:

$$x \times x \times x$$
$$\implies 50 \times 50 \times 50$$
$$\implies 50 \times 2500$$
$$\implies 125000$$

When evaluating $x \times x \times x$, the result of the computation doesn't rely on the order in which we evaluate it: we can do $(x \times x) \times x$ or $x \times (x \times x)$. However, computers like to follow rules exactly, so typically, the order is chosen when the expression is read into the computer, either leftmost first or rightmost first.

An expression like this, which depends on the value of a variable, is called a *function*. In this case, we've written a function that finds the cube of a number. So, let's name it:

$$\text{cube } x = x \times x \times x$$

Now, we can give the value of x explicitly, writing it out like this:

$$\text{cube } 50$$
$$\implies \quad 50 \times 50 \times 50$$
$$\implies \quad 50 \times 2500$$
$$\implies \quad 125000$$

In the first step, we substituted cube 50 with its definition. We can view the computation in tree form, too:

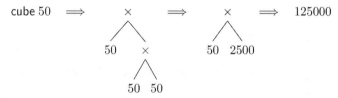

7.3 More operators

Let's introduce some more interesting operators in our expressions. We will introduce the = or equals operator and the special values *true* and *false* (not every value has to be a number). Now, we can write $x = 4$, and if x is indeed 4 in the current environment, we get *true*; otherwise, we get *false*. Here, = is the operator, and x and 4 are the *operands*. In the expression $1 + 2$, the operator is +, and the operands are 1 and 2.

Now, we can build a more complicated operator that can make a decision between two sub-expressions based on an equality test like this. For example, we may write

$$\text{if } x = 4 \text{ then } 0 \text{ else } x + 1$$

(This is only somewhat related to the `if ... then ... else` construct of chapter 4; please put that similarity out of your mind.) As a mathematical construct, this looks rather strange: we are used to seeing operators like + and ×, which consist of one symbol and have an operand on either side. This new operator has three parts (if, then, and else) and three operands ($x = 4$, 0, and $x + 1$), and they are spread all over the place! But if we write it out as a tree, it looks much like the earlier trees:

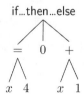

An operator having more than two operands is not so strange after all. Suppose we evaluate it in the environment where $x = 6$:

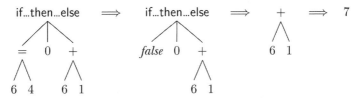

Of course, we can write it out in linear form:

$$\text{if } \underline{6 = 4} \text{ then 0 else } 6 + 1$$
$$\implies \text{if } \underline{\textit{false}} \text{ then 0 else } 6 + 1$$
$$\implies \underline{6 + 1}$$
$$\implies 7$$

And, we can name the function:

$$\text{test } l =$$
$$\text{if } x = 4 \text{ then 0 else } x + 1$$

We are getting a little closer to the sorts of calculations a real program does: making decisions about which part of an expression to evaluate based on input data and defining and using reusable functions.

7.4   A larger function

Now let's write a real, useful function. Given a number, say 4, it will calculate the *factorial*, written 4!, of the number. The factorial of a number is all the numbers from 1 to that number multiplied together. For example, the factorial of 4 is $4 \times 3 \times 2 \times 1$, which is 24. The number of possible orderings of a pack of playing cards is 52!, which is a very large number indeed. To calculate a factorial, we start at the given number, and we want to keep multiplying it by the number one smaller and one smaller and one smaller until we reach 1. Then, we want to stop rather than keep multiplying by 0, −1, −2, etc. You can see that we will have to use an if . . . then . . . else construct because we have a decision to make. Let's begin to define our function. The first part is easy: if the number is 1, the answer is 1:

$$\text{factorial } n =$$
$$\text{if } n = 1 \text{ then 1 else } \ldots$$

Now we must consider what to do when the number is greater than 1. In this case, we want to multiply the number by the factorial of the number one smaller since, for example, $4 \times 3 \times 2 \times 1 = 4 \times 3!$. So we write it out:

$$\text{factorial } n =$$

$$\text{if } n = 1 \text{ then } 1 \text{ else } n \times \text{factorial } (n-1)$$

Notice that our function uses itself within its own definition. This is not a problem as long as the computation eventually completes and gives a result. Here it is for the number 4:

$$\underline{\text{factorial } 4}$$

$\Longrightarrow$ if $\underline{4 = 1}$ then 1 else $4 \times$ factorial $(4 - 1)$

$\Longrightarrow$ if $\underline{\textit{false} \text{ then } 1 \text{ else } 4 \times \text{factorial } (4 - 1)}$

$\Longrightarrow$ $4 \times$ factorial $(\underline{4 - 1})$

$\Longrightarrow$ $4 \times \underline{\text{factorial } 3}$

$\Longrightarrow$ $4 \times ($if $\underline{3 = 1}$ then 1 else $3 \times$ factorial $(3 - 1))$

$\Longrightarrow$ $4 \times ($if $\underline{\textit{false} \text{ then } 1 \text{ else } 3 \ \times \text{factorial } (3 - 1)})$

$\Longrightarrow$ $4 \times (3 \times$ factorial $(\underline{3 - 1}))$

$\Longrightarrow$ $4 \times (3 \times \underline{\text{factorial } 2})$

$\Longrightarrow$ $4 \times (3 \times ($if $\underline{2 = 1}$ then 1 else $2 \times$ factorial $(2 - 1)))$

$\Longrightarrow$ $4 \times (3 \times ($if $\underline{\textit{false} \text{ then } 1 \text{ else } 2 \times \text{factorial } (2 - 1)}))$

$\Longrightarrow$ $4 \times (3 \times (2 \times$ factorial $(\underline{2 - 1})))$

$\Longrightarrow$ $4 \times (3 \times (2 \times \underline{\text{factorial } 1}))$

$\Longrightarrow$ $4 \times (3 \times (2 \times ($if $\underline{1 = 1}$ then 1 else $2 \times$ factorial $(1 - 1))))$

$\Longrightarrow$ $4 \times (3 \times (2 \times ($if $\underline{\textit{true} \text{ then } 1 \text{ else } 2 \times \text{factorial } (1 - 1)})))$

$\Longrightarrow$ $4 \times (3 \times (\underline{2 \times 1}))$

$\Longrightarrow$ $4 \times (\underline{3 \times 2})$

$\Longrightarrow$ $\underline{4 \times 6}$

$\Longrightarrow$ 24

We said earlier that we wanted the expression to get smaller with each step. This isn't the case here: we relax this restriction to say simply that in a properly working program with a proper input, the computation eventually finishes. Here is the tree for factorial:

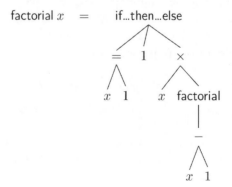

7.5   A second task

Consider another simple task with numbers. Given two numbers x and y, we wish to calculate x^y, which is pronounced "x to the power y". This is equal to x multiplied by itself y times. So, for example, $2^5 = 2 \times 2 \times 2 \times 2 \times 2 = 32$. On the other hand, $5^2 = 5 \times 5 = 25$. Note that it is a mathematical convention that any positive number to the power 0 is 1. This fact allows us to begin to write the power function (notice it has two inputs):

$$\text{power } x\ y =$$
$$\text{if } y = 0 \text{ then } 1 \text{ else} \ldots$$

However, if y is greater than 0, we want to calculate x times x^{y-1}:

$$\text{power } x\ y =$$
$$\text{if } y = 0 \text{ then } 1 \text{ else } x \times \text{power } x\ (y - 1)$$

So, we can now calculate 2^5, showing just the important steps:

$$\underline{\text{power } 2\ 5}$$
$$\implies \quad 2 \times \underline{\text{power } 2\ 4}$$
$$\implies \quad 2 \times (2 \times \underline{\text{power } 2\ 3})$$
$$\implies \quad 2 \times (2 \times (2 \times \underline{\text{power } 2\ 2}))$$
$$\implies \quad 2 \times (2 \times (2 \times (2 \times \underline{\text{power } 2\ 1})))$$
$$\implies \quad 2 \times (2 \times (2 \times (2 \times (2 \times \underline{\text{power } 2\ 0}))))$$
$$\implies \quad 2 \times (2 \times (2 \times (2 \times \underline{(2 \times 1)})))$$
$$\implies \quad 32$$

7.6   Lists

We have looked at numbers like 2 and 32 and the truth values *true* and *false*, but interesting programs often have to operate on more complicated structures. One such is a *list*, which we write with square brackets and commas, like this: [1, 5, 4]. A list is an ordered collection of other values. That is, the lists [1, 5, 4] and [5, 4, 1] are different, even though they contain the same values. An empty list [] contains no items. The first element of a list is called the *head*, and there is a built-in function to get at it:

$$\underline{\text{head } [1, 5, 4]}$$
$$\implies \quad 1$$

The rest of the elements are collectively referred to as the *tail*, and again there is a built-in function to retrieve it:

$$\underline{\text{tail } [1, 5, 4]}$$
$$\implies \quad [5, 4]$$

The empty list [] has neither a head nor a tail. We need just one more thing for our example programs, and that is the • operator, which sticks two lists together:

$$[1, 5, 4] \bullet [2, 3]$$
$$\implies \quad [1, 5, 4, 2, 3]$$

Let's write a function to find the length of a list using the tail function:

length l =
    if l = [] then 0 else 1 + length (tail l)

The empty list has length 0, and the length of any other list is 1 plus the length of its tail. Notice that the = operator works on lists, too. We can try a sample evaluation:

length [2, 3]
$\implies$ if [2, 3] = [] then 0 else 1 + length (tail [2, 3])
$\implies$ if *false* then 0 else 1 + length (tail [2, 3])
$\implies$ 1 + length (tail [2, 3])
$\implies$ 1 + length [3]
$\implies$ 1 + if [3] = [] then 0 else 1 + length (tail [3])
$\implies$ 1 + if *false* then 0 else 1 + length (tail [3])
$\implies$ 1 + (1 + length (tail [3]))
$\implies$ 1 + (1 + length [])
$\implies$ 1 + (1 + if [] = [] then 0 else 1 + length (tail l))
$\implies$ 1 + (1 + if *false* then 0 else 1 + length (tail l))
$\implies$ 1 + (1 + 0)
$\implies$ 1 + 1
$\implies$ 2

These diagrams are becoming a little unwieldy, so as we write more complicated functions, we will leave some of the detail out, concentrating on the repeated uses of the main function we are writing (here, length):

length [2, 3]
$\implies$ 1 + length [3]
$\implies$ 1 + (1 + length [])
$\implies$ 1 + (1 + 0)
$\implies$ 2

Much better. We can modify our function easily to calculate the sum of a list of numbers:

sum $l =$
$\quad$ if $l = [\,]$ then 0 else head $l +$ sum (tail l)

$$
\begin{array}{rl}
& \underline{\text{sum } [9,\, 1,\, 302]} \\
\Longrightarrow & 9 + \underline{\text{sum } [1,\, 302]} \\
\Longrightarrow & 9 + (1 + \underline{\text{sum } [302]}) \\
\Longrightarrow & 9 + (1 + (302 + \underline{\text{sum } [\,]})) \\
\Longrightarrow & \underline{9 + (1 + (302 + 0))} \\
\Longrightarrow & 312
\end{array}
$$

Time for something a little more ambitious. How can we reverse a list? For example, we want reverse $[1, 3, 5, 7]$ to give $[7, 5, 3, 1]$. Remember that we only have access to the first element of a list (the head) and the list, which forms the tail of a given list; we do not have a direct way to access the end of the list. This prevents us from simply repeatedly taking the last element of the list and building a new one with the • operator (which, you recall, sticks two lists together). Well, we can at least write out the part for the empty list since reversing the empty list just gives the empty list:

reverse $l =$
$\quad$ if $l = [\,]$ then $[\,]$ else . . .

If the list is not empty, it has a head and a tail. We want to make the head go at the end of the final list, and before that, we want the rest of the list reversed. So we write

reverse $l =$
$\quad$ if $l = [\,]$ then $[\,]$ else reverse (tail l) • [head l]

Notice that we wrote [head l] rather than just head l because we need to turn it into a list so that the • operator can work. Let's check that it works (again, in our shortened form of a diagram):

$$
\begin{array}{rl}
& \underline{\text{reverse } [1,\, 2,\, 3]} \\
\Longrightarrow & \underline{\text{reverse } [2,\, 3]} \bullet [1] \\
\Longrightarrow & (\underline{\text{reverse } [3]} \bullet [2]) \bullet [1] \\
\Longrightarrow & (([3] \bullet \underline{\text{reverse } [\,]}) \bullet [2]) \bullet [1] \\
\Longrightarrow & ((\underline{[3] \bullet [\,]}) \bullet [2]) \bullet [1] \\
\Longrightarrow & [3,\, 2,\, 1]
\end{array}
$$

7.7   *Sorting a list*

Let's approach a more complicated problem. How might we sort a list into numerical order from whatever order it is in to start with? For example, we want to sort [53, 9, 2, 6, 19] to produce [2, 6, 9, 19, 53]. The problem is a little unapproachable and seems rather complex. One way to begin is to see whether we can solve the simplest part of the problem. Well, just like for reverse, sorting a list of length zero is easy—there is nothing to do:

$$\text{sort } l =$$
$$\text{if } l = [] \text{ then } [] \text{ else} \dots$$

If the list has a length greater than zero, it has a head and a tail. Assume for a moment that the tail is already sorted. Then, we just need to insert the head into the tail at the correct position, and the whole list will be sorted. The following is a definition for sort, assuming we have an insert function (we will concoct insert in a moment):

$$\text{sort } l =$$
$$\text{if } l = [] \text{ then } [] \text{ else insert (head } l) \text{ (sort (tail } l))$$

If the list is empty, we do nothing; otherwise, we insert the head of the list into its sorted tail. Assuming insert exists, the following is the whole evaluation of our sorting procedure on the list [53, 9, 2, 6, 19], showing only uses of sort and insert for brevity:

sort [53, 9, 2, 6, 19]
$\implies$ insert 53 (sort [9, 2, 6, 19])
$\implies$ insert 53 (insert 9 (sort [2, 6, 19]))
$\implies$ insert 53 (insert 9 (insert 2 (sort [6, 19])))
$\implies$ insert 53 (insert 9 (insert 2 (insert 6 (sort [19]))))
$\implies$ insert 53 (insert 9 (insert 2 (insert 6 (insert 19 (sort [])))))
$\implies$ insert 53 (insert 9 (insert 2 (insert 6 (insert 19 []))))
$\implies$ insert 53 (insert 9 (insert 2 (insert 6 [19])))
$\implies$ insert 53 (insert 9 (insert 2 [6, 19]))
$\implies$ insert 53 (insert 9 [2, 6, 19])
$\implies$ insert 53 [2, 6, 9, 19]
$\implies$ [2, 6, 9, 19, 53]

Now, we must define insert. It is a function that takes two things: the item x to be inserted and the (already-sorted) list l in which to insert it. If the list is empty, we can simply build the list [x]:

$$\text{insert } x \, l =$$
$$\text{if } l = [] \text{ then } [x] \text{ else} \ldots$$

There are two other cases. If x is less than or equal to the head of the list, we can just put it at the front of the list, and we are done:

$$\text{insert } x \, l =$$
$$\text{if } l = [] \text{ then } [x] \text{ else}$$
$$\text{if } x \le \text{head } l \text{ then } [x] \bullet l \text{ else} \ldots$$

Otherwise, we have not yet found an appropriate place for our number, and we must keep searching. The result should be our head, followed by the insertion of our number in the tail:

$$\text{insert } x \, l =$$
$$\text{if } l = [] \text{ then } [x] \text{ else}$$
$$\text{if } x \le \text{head } l \text{ then } [x] \bullet l \text{ else}$$
$$[\text{head } l] \bullet \text{insert } x \, (\text{tail } l)$$

Consider the evaluation of insert 3 [1, 1, 2, 3, 5, 9]:

$$\text{insert } 3 \, [1, 1, 2, 3, 5, 9]$$
$$\implies [1] \bullet \text{insert } 3 \, [1, 2, 3, 5, 9]$$
$$\implies [1] \bullet ([1] \bullet \text{insert } 3 \, [2, 3, 5, 9])$$
$$\implies [1] \bullet ([1] \bullet ([2] \bullet \text{insert } 3 \, [3, 5, 9]))$$
$$\implies [1] \bullet ([1] \bullet ([2] \bullet ([3] \bullet [3, 5, 9])))$$
$$\implies [1, 1, 2, 3, 3, 5, 9]$$

We compare 3 to 1. Too large. We compare it with the second 1. Too large. We compare it with 2. Again, too large. We compare it with 3. It is equal, so we have found a place for it. The rest of the list need not be dealt with now, and the list is sorted. The following is the whole program in one place:

$$\text{insert } x \, l =$$
$$\text{if } l = [] \text{ then } [x] \text{ else}$$
$$\text{if } x \le \text{head } l \text{ then } [x] \bullet l \text{ else}$$
$$[\text{head } l] \bullet \text{insert } x \, (\text{tail } l)$$

$$\text{sort } l =$$
$$\text{if } l = [] \text{ then } [] \text{ else insert } (\text{head } l) \, (\text{sort } (\text{tail } l))$$

In this chapter, we have covered a lot of ground, going from the simplest mathematical expressions to a complicated computer program. Doing the problems should help you to fill in the gaps. In the next chapter, we return to higher-level topics, newly mindful of the underlying mechanism they all share.

Problems

For solutions, see appendix B.

1 Evaluate the following simple expressions following normal mathematical rules and adding parentheses where needed. Show each evaluation in both tree and textual form:

(a) $1+1+1$

(b) $2 \times 2 \times 2$

(c) $2 \times 3 + 4$

2 In an environment in which $x = 4$, $y = 5$, and $z = 100$, evaluate the following expressions:

(a) $x \times x \times y$

(b) $z \times y + z$

(c) $z \times z$

3 Consider the following function, which has two inputs—x and y:

$$f\, x\, y = x \times y \times x$$

Evaluate the following expressions:

(a) f 4 5

(b) f (f 4 5) 5

(c) f (f 4 5) (f 5 4)

4 Recall the truth values *true* and *false* and the if. . .then. . .else construction. Evaluate the following expressions:

(a) f 5 4 = f 4 5

(b) if 1 = 2 then 3 else 4

(c) if (if 1 = 2 then *false* else *true*) then 3 else 4

5 Evaluate the following list expressions:

(a) head [2,3,4]

(b) tail [2]

(c) [head [2,3,4]] • [2,3,4]

6 Consider this function, which removes elements in positions 2, 4, 6 . . . from a list, leaving elements in positions 1, 3, 5 . . .

$$\text{odds}\, l =$$

$$\text{if}\, l = [\,]\, \text{then}\, [\,]\, \text{else}$$

$$\text{if tail } l = [] \text{ then } l \text{ else}$$
$$[\text{head } l] \bullet \text{odds (tail (tail } x))$$

Evaluate the following uses of this function:

(a) odds []

(b) odds [1,2]

(c) odds [1,2,3]

You need not show all the stages of evaluation if you can do it in your head.

Summary

- Simple arithmetic turns out not to be so simple after all. Humans and computers have differing ideas of what is simple and what is difficult.
- In addition to arithmetic, we build programs by making choices among alternative paths, defining our own functions, and introducing structured data such as lists.
- The entirety of our computer's operation can be built from just these simple building blocks, storing and processing data for any task and communicating with the user and other computers.

Gray areas

This chapter covers

- Historical methods for printing pictures and reproducing photographs using only black ink and white paper
- Computer methods for printing pictures and reproducing photographs using halftoning and dithering

With only black ink and white paper, we can draw both beautiful letters and good line drawings, such as the diagrams of Bézier curves from chapter 2. But what about reproducing photographs? How can we create the intermediate gray tones using only black ink and white paper? In this chapter, we will look at precomputer methods for the reproduction of gray tones and then see how computers can automate the process.

8.1 Simple thresholding

Consider the two images in figure 8.1: a photograph of a camel and a rather higher-resolution picture of a smooth gradient between black and white. We will use these pictures to compare the different methods of reproduction we discuss. From looking at the page (at least if you are reading this book in physical form rather than on a

Figure 8.1   Our two example images: a photograph and a gradient

computer screen), you can see that it is indeed possible, at least when one views the page from a normal reading distance. But how?

The simplest method of converting a gray image into a black and white one is simply to pick a level of gray above which we consider each part of the image black and below which we consider it white. Figure 8.2 is our camel, printed using black ink for any part that is more than 50% black (i.e., a mid-gray) and no ink for any part that is less than 50% black.

Well, we can see the shape of the camel, but the result is less than spectacular. Let's try moving the threshold to 40%, as shown in figure 8.3. We can't see as much detail of the camel in this case, but at least its legs are solid. If we move the other way, to a threshold of 60%, things get even worse, as shown in figure 8.4.

Figure 8.2   Thresholding at 50%   **Figure 8.3   Thresholding at 40%**   **Figure 8.4   Thresholding at 60%**

If we have to manually pick a suitable threshold for each image in a book to get even an acceptable result, the process is going to be time consuming. Figure 8.5 shows our black-to-white gradient at 40%, 50%, and 60% thresholds. These images bear almost no resemblance to the original.

Figure 8.5   Our gradient at three thresholds: 40%, 50%, and 60%

8.2   *Historical methods*

Before describing some more advanced methods for gray tone reproduction, like the one used to make the images at the beginning of this chapter, we will take a brief historical detour: the problem of reproducing gray tones is not intrinsically one of computer printing but has been important in newspaper and print production for hundreds of years.

The process of printing is essentially one of duplication. In former times, if we wanted just one of something, we could have a painter paint it or a scribe write it down. We might even be able to produce a few thousand bibles by having monks copy them repeatedly for years at a time. However, we could not produce a million copies of a newspaper, with text and pictures, overnight, no matter how extensive our resources. To produce text, we require only black ink on white paper. To reproduce paintings and photographs, we need methods that provide the illusion of gray tones. Printing the paper dozens of times with diluted inks to form multiple shades of gray, as the watercolorist would, is time consuming and physically difficult—think of the amount of water that would end up on the paper, for one. So we must find other ways. Figure 8.6 shows a very simple scheme for creating an illusion of gray on a display such as a computer screen.

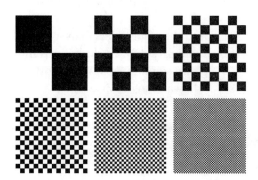

Figure 8.6   Approximating gray with checkerboards

We have a checkerboard pattern of black and white, and if we get the scale small enough, the viewer stands far enough away, or both, the appearance is of a mid-gray. Put this book on a stand and walk slowly away. How far do you have to go for each of the parts of this picture to appear gray? Similar techniques can work when printing on paper, but we have to account for the spreading of ink and all the other imperfections of the physical world.

Some of the earliest reproduction methods involved cutting patterns into wooden blocks, applying ink, and stamping them onto cloth or paper either by hand or in a primitive press. The process is similar to a child cutting a potato to make a stamp: the wood is removed in areas where the artist does not want ink, and then ink is applied to the raised portions. Figure 8.7 shows a woodblock print *Der Formschneider* (The Blockcutter) from the *Panoplia omnium illiberalium mechanicarum* (Book of Trades), published in Germany in 1568.

The detail achievable depends upon the closeness of the grain of the wood, the properties of the ink and paper, and the permeability of the wood to ink. Attempts to produce areas that appear gray by using hatching or other patterns are likely to be too coarse to be convincing, or they result in a solid inked area due to ink spreading across the surface of the block or along the fibers of the paper.

The term *intaglio* (in-<u>tah</u>-lee-o), from the Italian *intagliare* (to engrave) refers to a group of techniques in which a metal plate has material removed manually, is rubbed with viscous ink all over, has the excess removed carefully with a cloth, and is then pressed onto a dampened piece of paper. The ink remains only in the lines engraved in the plate and is transferred to the paper by the pressure of the press. Thus, the removal of material is normally done in the opposite sense to that in the woodblock

Figure 8.7 Woodblock print. Der Formschneider (The Blockcutter), 1568.

process: we engrave where we want ink to be present, not where we want it to be absent.

The term *engraving* in the context of printing refers to the use of the tools traditionally used for engraving decoration on, for example, decorative silverwork, on metal plates instead, which are then used for printing. Decorative metal engravers had used more primitive versions of this technique to "print" their work-in-progress when designing *niello*, a type of decoration where engraved lines were filled with a black substance and polished for contrast. Making proof prints with ink helped to show what the final design might look like when blacked.

In the late 15th century, engraving began to be used for the reproduction of simplified versions of paintings and for original works. A copper plate would be inscribed with a hard metal tool known as a *burin*. The plate could then be used to produce hundreds of copies of a print. (Given that copper is soft and the printing is done under pressure, it would eventually produce faded prints.) Engraving was a highly skilled and difficult process. Figure 8.8, featuring *Ars moriendi* by Master ES from 1450, is a relatively early, simple, and coarse engraving. Figure 8.9, featuring *Melancolia I* by the German master Albrecht Düreris, is a much more accomplished and fine engraving.

Alternative intaglio methods were developed, hoping to improve the fineness of the result or lessen the amount of expertise required. The *mezzotint* method, from the Italian "mezzo tinto" meaning "half-painted," involves using a device called a rocker to roughen the plate all over. Ink gathers in the little indentations made by such a process, leading to an entirely black image. Burnishing tools are then used to flatten the copper in areas where ink is not wanted. Because this process is gradual (one may burnish

Figure 8.8   Engraving. Ars moriendi by Master ES, circa 1450.

Figure 8.9   Fine engraving. Melacolia I, Albrecht Dürer, 1514.

more or less), the illusion of shades is easier to achieve. Figure 8.10 shows a mezzotint plate being wiped off, ready for printing.

Figure 8.10   Wiping excess ink from a mezzotint plate. (Photo courtesy of David Ladmore)

Unfortunately, due to the softness of copper and the smallness of the indentations, these plates did not last long, and the quality of the printing declined with each pressing. Figure 8.11 shows a mezzotint print. Note the fineness of the gray tone reproduction.

Another alternative to engraving is the process of *etching*, in which the whole plate is covered in an acid-resistant substance, which is then scratched off using tools in areas where the artist wants ink to appear in the final print. The plate is then washed with acid, which roughens the metal in unprotected areas so that they will hold ink. The plate is then printed as with any other intaglio process. The great advantage is that

Figure 8.11 A mezzotint print. "Sunshine Falling on a Door," by Danish artist Peter Ilsted (1861–1933)

the process is available to the general artist, who can draw in this medium without learning the difficult metalwork skills of the engraver. Improvements to the process include "stopping out," where the plate is briefly dipped in the acid, more acid-resistant substance is added to certain areas, and then the plate is dipped again. This process allows better control over gray tones. Figure 8.12 is an etching by Rembrandt, known as *The Hundred Guilder Print*, named after the sum reportedly once paid for a copy.

Figure 8.12 Etching. Christ Healing the Sick, or The Hundred Guilder Print, by Rembrandt van Rijn, c. 1647–1649.

It might surprise you that even the photographic process has trouble representing gray tones. Photographic film consists of particles of compounds of silver suspended in a gel. When exposed to light, tiny changes to the crystal structure record an invisible image. When developed, each particle is either converted to silver (which will appear black in the final photograph) or not converted (which will appear white). The process of enlarging the photograph from the negative to the positive paper print may introduce grays by dint of its analogue nature, of course, but if enlarged enough, one can see the so-called film grain clearly. Figure 8.13 shows an enlargement of a photograph of a plain gray card. Under a powerful electron microscope, in figure 8.14, we can see the individual crystals on the photographic film.

Figure 8.13   Film grain. (Photo courtesy of Keith Cooper)

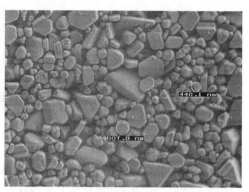

Figure 8.14   Film under an electron microscope. (Photo courtesy of University of Rochester)

None of the methods we have seen so far allow for the automatic conversion of photographic content to a printable form, such as a plate that might be wanted for a daily newspaper. We have a gray-tone image in the form of a photographic negative. Our printing process, however, allows only black and white, so we wish to automatically convert the gray tones to a series of regularly spaced dots whose diameter reflects the level of gray. Figure 8.15 shows our gradient, followed by its so-called *halftone*.

Figure 8.15   Our gradient and its halftone

You can see that the spacing of the dots is quite wide and that they can be quite large: this is counterintuitive but deliberate. By making sure that the dots are properly separated, we make the image easily reproducible, even on cheap, porous newsprint. Perhaps 50 to 80 lines of dots per inch is sufficient. For higher-quality coated paper used in book production, we might be able to go as far as 150 lines per inch (lpi).

Early methods of halftone production involved placing a device known as a halftone screen in front of photographic paper and projecting the original image through it with the use of a camera lens. The first halftone screens were made in about 1850 from a fine cloth gauze by the British scientist William Henry Fox Talbot (1800–1877). Later, they were commercially manufactured from glass engraved with a grid of lines. The effect of these is, through optical effects, to project a halftone image—a series of distinct dots of varying size—onto the photographic paper. This can then be used as the starting point for producing plates for printing. The image has successfully been reduced to only black and white through purely physical means. Figure 8.16 shows one of the earliest halftoned pictures in mass production: it shows Steinway Hall on East 14th Street in Manhattan, printed in the *Daily Graphic* on December 2, 1873. This was the first method of printing a photograph directly from the negative with no manual intervention.

Figure 8.16   Halftone of the Steinway Hall, printed in the Daily Graphic, December 2, 1873

8.3   *Digital halftoning*

Returning to computer science, we can simulate the halftone screen in software to produce the appropriate dot pattern for printing. Consider the three versions of our camel picture in figure 8.17. The first one, with the smallest dots, seems to have the highest effective sharpness and visual resolution. However, as the maximum dot size increases, so does the number of possible shades. The middle image, when viewed at a distance, is in fact a closer representation of the original image. The last one has yet more sizes of dots (thus, effective gray levels), but the resolution is now too coarse. We turn to our gradient for another look, printed in the same halftones as the camel pictures, as shown in figure 8.18.

Figure 8.17   Small, medium, and large halftone dots

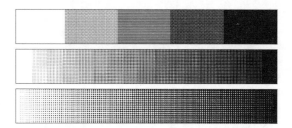

Figure 8.18   Fine, medium, and coarse halftones

At the top of figure 8.18 is the finest halftone; at the bottom, the coarsest. We can see that the larger number of apparent grays in the coarser dots is an advantage in this case: the top line looks very fragmented indeed. At a distance, the middle and bottom are both good.

We can perform this halftoning by producing patterns that look like increasing sizes of ink dots. These patterns can then be displayed on screen or printed. To do this, we divide the image up into little 2×2 or 4×4 squares of pixels and then choose one of a set of patterns to represent the average level of gray in the square. The result is a picture with the same number of pixels, but where each is black or white. Figure 8.19 shows the patterns for a 2×2 scheme.

Figure 8.19   Halftone dots 2 × 2

Notice that there are five patterns, not four as we might expect. We use the first pattern for a gray level between 0% and 20%; the second, between 20% and 40%; and so forth. In this scheme, we have tried to keep the black dots adjacent to one another to build up little spots, which is better suited to the spreading behavior of ink on paper. The process is known as *dithering*. The patterns may be generated by listing the order in which they turn black in a table:

$$1 \quad 2$$
$$3 \quad 4$$

So, for the third pattern, we blacken all pixels with values less than 3 (that is, 1 and 2). It is known as an *ordered dither* for this reason. Figure 8.20 shows the result.

Figure 8.20   Our pictures using the 2 × 2 halftone

We only have five different shades of gray, and the image suffers for it: we can see areas that in the original image were subtly shaded as plain, flat sections—not a good result. Let's double the length of the side of our square to 4. Now, we will have $4 \times 4 + 1 = 17$ different levels of gray, but the image will have fewer dots overall. Will the increase in the number of shades outweigh the decrease in apparent resolution? Here is the generating table:

$$
\begin{array}{cccc}
15 & 10 & 8 & 14 \\
5 & 1 & 2 & 12 \\
11 & 3 & 4 & 6 \\
13 & 7 & 9 & 16 \\
\end{array}
$$

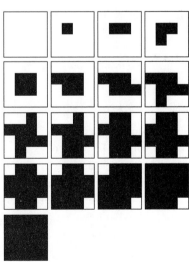

Figure 8.21 is the resultant 17 dither patterns. Again, they form a cohesive spot and are built up somewhat symmetrically.

As the tone moves from white to black, the spot grows gradually. If you imagine the patterns tiled repeatedly across the page, you can see that as the black spot grows, the white sections left in the corners form white spots. Thus, we have a smooth transition. Figure 8.22 is the result of dithering with these patterns for the camel and the gradient.

Figure 8.21   Patterns for a 4 × 4 halftone

Figure 8.22   Our pictures using the 4 × 4 halftone

Prop this book up against a wall, retreat to the other side of the room (or perhaps halfway), and see which looks more camel-like. What about at a normal reading distance? Such halftone patterns are used in most modern printing. Figure 8.23 provides microscope pictures of the camel as it is printed at the head of this chapter at 20× and 400× magnification.

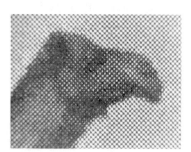
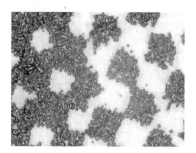

Figure 8.23   Our camel printed at high quality at 20× and 400× magnifications

For color images, several halftone screens are used, one for each of the primary printing colors used in the particular printing technology—often cyan, magenta, yellow, and black. The halftones are at different angles so that the colors do not interfere with one another and the ink is more evenly distributed. Figure 8.24 shows part of a glossy color leaflet at 20× and 400× magnification.

When we are producing a result for a type of device that has reasonably sharp or predictable dots (such as a computer monitor) and none of the vagaries of ink-flow, we can choose a more appropriate ordered dither. We are free of the need to build a spot as such, leading to the appearance of a higher resolution. Black-and-white computer

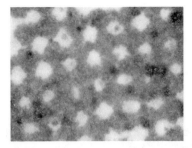

Figure 8.24   Multiple halftone screens at differing angles for color reproduction (20× and 400×)

displays are rather rare these days but were common in the past. Consider the table and pattern for the 2 × 2 case given in figure 8.25.

We still have five levels of gray, but the apparent resolution should be higher, and the eye should find it harder to discern individual dots since we try to keep them as small as possible for as long as possible. Figure 8.26 shows the camel and gradient drawn with this new set of patterns.

Figure 8.25   A different table for 2 × 2 halftoning

Figure 8.26   Our images using the new 2 × 2 table

Figure 8.27 is a similarly constructed 4 × 4 pattern giving, as before, 17 grays. Notice that it is built in such a way as to keep the spots as small as possible.

This time, the results are rather better due to the increased number of dot patterns, which allow a wider range of apparent shades of gray to be reproduced. Figure 8.28 shows our camel and gradient built with the 4 × 4 patterns generated from our table.

The spots are, in general, much smaller than in the first set of patterns we looked at, and the gradient is reasonably convincing, although it does appear to be divided into

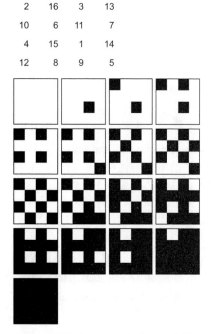

Figure 8.27   A 4 × 4 table for small dots and its dither patterns

Figure 8.28   Our example images with the small-dot 4 × 4 pattern

little blocks. Figure 8.29 shows our camel picture using these sorts of small-dot dither patterns of sizes 2 × 2, 4 × 4, and 8 × 8. The difference is even more obvious when we use the gradient, as in figure 8.30.

Figure 8.29   Small-spot ordered dithers with 2 × 2, 4 × 4, and 8 × 8 patterns

8.4   *Better dithering*

Our small-dot ordered dither patterns, suitable for onscreen use where pixels are clearly defined (unlike ink on paper), are not too bad. They do the job of creating

Figure 8.30 Small-spot ordered dithers with 2 × 2, 4 × 4, and 8 × 8 patterns

the impression of gray shades where only black and white exist. However, the regular patterns of dots can be distracting: we see those patterns instead of the image since our eyes are drawn to regular features. The technique of *error diffusion* leads to a better result than ordered dithering, with fewer distracting patterns. This method was invented in 1976 by Robert W. Floyd and his student Louis Steinberg at Stanford University. Say that we have an image made up of grays between 0% ink (white) and 100% ink (black) like the one in this diagram; unavoidably, we will have to use a somewhat small example:

```
50   20   70
40   30   70
50   40   90
```

We proceed pixel by pixel, starting at the top left, dealing with a row of pixels in order, and then moving on to the next row until we have looked at the whole image. For each pixel, we first decide whether to paint it black or white in the final image. If it is 50% or more black, we make that pixel black; if it is less than 50%, we make it white. We write this value to the final image. Now we consider the error inherent in that choice: How much too white or too black were we forced to make the pixel due to only having fully white and fully black available? For example, on the first pixel, we would choose to place a 100% black pixel, and the original value was 50%, so we were forced to make it 50% too black. We redistribute this error to some of the surrounding pixels of the original image according to the following proportions chosen by Floyd and Steinberg (where × marks the current pixel):

```
        ×        7/16
3/16   5/16    1/16
```

So, for our first pixel, the error of −50% is distributed among the surrounding pixels in the following amounts:

```
        ×        −22%
−9%    −16%    −3%
```

We apply this arithmetic to the original image to obtain the following values:

```
100   -2   70
31    14   67
50    40   90
```

Now we can move on to the next pixel and so on, all across the first row and onto the next, until the image is wholly dealt with. The end result should be that the final image only has the values 0 and 100, so it has been successfully reduced to just black and white. The overall average gray level of the image should be the same because the errors have been only moved around, not forgotten about (except at the edge of the image, where the errors "fall off"). Here is the end result for our image:

```
100   0   100
0     0   100
100   0   100
```

A useful feature of this scheme is that a flat mid-gray at 50% will produce a stable, miniature checkerboard pattern, which is not distracting since it is so small. Consider the following original:

```
50   50   50
50   50   50
50   50   50
```

The final image, after each pixel has been processed, will have the following pattern of black and white pixels:

```
100   0     100
0     100   0
100   0     100
```

Figure 8.31 shows our camel picture and gradient processed with the algorithm we just discussed.

You can see that there appear to be much finer gradations of gray, and while the eye can discern some patterns in the flat, shaded areas, they are much less distracting than in the case of the ordered dither. Overall, we have a much more pleasing result. The gradient is much finer too, especially when viewed from a distance. There are several newer variations of this procedure, using more complicated diffusion of errors.

Figure 8.31 **Floyd–Steinberg dithering of our two example images**

Problems

For solutions, see appendix B. Templates for you to photocopy or print out for problems 8.1–8.3 are available in appendix C.

Show the 17 dither patterns generated from each of these grids of numbers:

1

1	9	3	11
13	5	15	7
4	12	2	10
16	8	14	6

2

1	9	13	3
16	5	7	11
12	8	6	15
4	14	10	2

3

2	6	11	15
4	8	9	13
14	10	7	3
16	12	5	1

Summary

- Just as black shapes on white paper can be used to draw text and images, so can the same black ink on the same white paper simulate grayscale images.
- Similar mechanisms can be used to simulate grayscale images on black-and-white computer displays (for example, early eBook readers).

- Hundreds of years of precomputer efforts, from medieval woodblock printing to halftone newspaper photographs, show how difficult the problem of grayscale reproduction is.
- Computer methods range from the simplistic (thresholding) to the sophisticated (digital halftoning and Floyd–Steinberg dithering).
- These methods also apply to reproducing color images from a small number of inks or digital images on screens with few colors.

A typeface

A page's content is made up of tiny little filled shapes, one for each letter, number, or piece of punctuation. The shapes are taken from what is known as a typeface or font. In this chapter, we will choose for an example the typeface Palatino, designed in 1950 by the legendary German typographer Hermann Zapf (1918–2015). The definitive modern version of Palatino from Linotype of Germany contains some 1,328 *glyphs* (shapes for characters) for each typeface in the family (Roman [normal], *Italic*, **Bold**, and ***Bold Italic***), a total of 5,312 shapes for the typeface designer to draw. You can see why commissioning a new typeface is expensive and so why buying high-quality typefaces for your own use can be expensive, too.

9.1 Introducing Palatino

Owing to its wealth of characters, Palatino Linotype supports many Western languages by providing appropriate accents and alternative glyphs in a single typeface, as shown in figure 9.1.

Afrikaans	Estonian	Latvian	Serbian
Albanian	Faroese	Lithuanian	Slovak
Basque	Finnish	Macedonian	Slovenian
Belarusian	French	Malay	Somali
Bulgarian	Galician	Maltese	Spanish
Catalan	German	Manx	Swahili
Cornish	Hungarian	Norwegian Bokmål	Swedish
Croatian	Icelandic	Norwegian Nynorsk	Swiss German
Czech	Indonesian	Oromo	Uzbek
Danish	Irish	Polish	Vietnamese
Dutch	Italian	Portuguese	Welsh
English	Kalaallisut	Romanian	Zulu
Esperanto	Kazakh	Russian	

Figure 9.1   **Languages supported in Palatino**

In addition, it contains the Cyrillic characters as well as those used in Modern Greek as well as the so-called Latin ones we use in English. Figure 9.2 shows the capital letters and lowercase letters used in English.

ABCDEFGHIJK
LMNOPQRSTU
VWXYZ

abcdefghijk
lmnopqrstu
vwxyz

Figure 9.2   **Capital and lowercase letters in Palatino**

Figure 9.3 shows the two styles of numbers, the so-called *lining numbers*, which have the same height as capital letters and all sit on the baseline, and the *old-style numbers*, some of which have descenders and are not all the same height as capital letters.

0123456789

0123456789

Figure 9.3   Two styles of numbers in Palatino

Figure 9.4 shows some of the *ligatures* available in Palatino. These are special glyphs used when letters would otherwise join unpleasantly or in other situations where two letters should be represented by a single glyph. Some are for decoration (such as Q followed by *u*, which is normally just *Qu*). Others look like ligatures but are really a different sound or letter (for example, a diphthong, such as œ).

IJ Qu Th æœ
fi fl ff ffi ffl fk ffk fj
sp st tt tz ch ck ct

Figure 9.4   Ligatures in Palatino

Next are the small caps, shown in figure 9.5, which are capital letters set to the same height as lowercase letters. Notice that the small caps are not just scaled-down versions of the ordinary capitals—having the same general weight, they may be used alongside them.

SMALL CAPS

Figure 9.5   Small caps in Palatino

Figure 9.6 provides accented letters, of which only a tiny portion are shown here. Accents attach in different places on each letter, so many typefaces contain an accented version of each common letter–accent pair, together with separate accent marks, which can be combined with other letters as required for more esoteric uses.

Figure 9.6   Accented letters in Palatino

Finally, figure 9.7 shows some of the many other glyphs in Palatino, for currency symbols and so forth, and some of the punctuation.

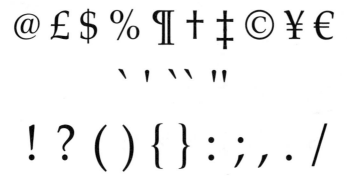

Figure 9.7   Symbols in Palatino

9.2   *Glyphs and metrics*

How do we pick letters from the typeface and place them on the page? Each glyph contains not only the lines and curves we have discussed earlier in the book, but also what are known as *metrics*: that is, a set of numbers governing how a letter relates to previous letters horizontally and where it lies vertically. Various numbers can be used to fit letters together pleasingly. The most important metrics are the *baseline* and the *advancement*. The baseline is just like the line on a schoolchild's ruled paper: capital letters sit on it, and letters with descenders like *g* and *y* drop somewhat below it. Every glyph is defined in relation to this baseline, so we can place it in the correct vertical position. The advancement tells us how much to move to the right after drawing the glyph—that is, how far the origin has moved. So, at the beginning of a line, we start at an *x* coordinate of 0 and move rightward by the advancement each time. Figure 9.8 shows three glyphs, defining various metrics. Some are needed for placing them on the page, and some information is used for other purposes.

The position of the letters in a line depends not only on the individual characters (the letter *i* is much narrower than the letter *w*, for example), but on the combinations

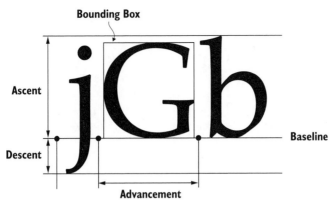

Figure 9.8 Glyph metrics

in which they are printed. For example, a capital *V* following a capital *A* looks odd if the spacing is not tightened, as seen in figure 9.9.

Figure 9.9 Overlapping letters for a more pleasing layout

In the example in figure 9.9, there is no tightening in the left-hand example, but tightening has been applied to the right-hand one. Such tightening is called *kerning*. The following are some of the rules from Palatino showing how much extra space is added or removed when the characters *A, a, :,* etc. follow the character *V.*

```
V A -111       V hyphen -74      V r -92
V a -92        V i -55           V semicolon -55
V colon -55    V o -111          V u -92
V comma -129   V period -129     V y -92
V e -111       V A -111          V Oslash -37
V OE -37       V ae -148         V oslash -130
V oe -130      V Aring -130      V quoteright 28
```

Figure 9.10 Kerning rules

The numbers are expressed in thousandths of a point. For example, you can see that when a hyphen follows a *V*, the hyphen is placed 74/1000 of a point closer to the *V* for a 1pt size font and 12 times that for a 12pt font, for example. Kerning is especially important when letters meet punctuation. Palatino has, in all, 1,031 such rules for pairs of characters. Overlapping of adjacent letters can also be achieved simply by extending the shape of the character beyond its bounding box. Figure 9.11 shows the particularly striking overlaps used by the various alternative glyphs available in another of Zapf's creations, the script-like Zapfino.

Figure 9.11   Alternative glyphs in Zapfino

The diagram shows various alternative glyphs for *d* and *g* in the Zapfino typeface. You can see that some suit the word more than others. In particular, in the bottom-right example, the initial *d* clashes with the next letter.

9.3   *Different sizes and shapes*

Before computers, when type was set manually using little metal pieces arranged into rows, smeared in ink, and pressed onto paper, it was natural for a typeface to have slightly different glyph designs for each size. A headline would have a subtly different character design to normal-sized text and, again, different to the sort of tiny text used for footnotes. Part of this setup is due to the essential optical characteristics of small shapes: for example, it is easier to read a small typeface if it has proportionally wider characters than its normal size. Part of it has to do with the physical characteristics of the ink and paper: ink spreads, and the way it spreads leads to the same metal shape showing differently at different sizes.

When designing a typeface by computer, however, it is tempting to take a shortcut: design the typeface once and then automatically scale it to whatever size is needed by simple arithmetic on its coordinates. Now, we have any size available, and designing the typeface is cheaper. This shortcut was not available to the metal type manufacturer. However, many good modern computer typefaces still have multiple so-called *optical sizes*. They may have separate shapes for 5pt, 8pt, 10pt, 12pt, and 16pt, for example. We can use the computer-scaling method in between sizes to obtain 11pt, for example. Figure 9.12, at the top, shows a phrase printed in the Latin Modern typeface at five different sizes. At the bottom of the figure, the same phrase is repeated but scaled up to show the differences clearly.

We have not yet looked at the other three faces of the Palatino typeface: the **Bold**, the *Italic*, and the ***Bold Italic***. A bold typeface is thicker and uses more ink. The italic has a different, sloping shape. Both are used for emphasis. The various shapes are designed to work comfortably together.

Optical Font Sizes
Optical Font Sizes
Optical Font Sizes
Optical Font Sizes
Optical Font Sizes

Optical Font Sizes
Optical Font Sizes
Optical Font Sizes
Optical Font Sizes
Optical Font Sizes

Figure 9.12   Optical font sizes in Latin Modern

Shape **Shape**

Shape Shape

Figure 9.13   Font shapes

You can see in figure 9.13 that the Italic has an entirely different shape from the Roman. This is usual for *serif* typefaces such as Palatino. (Serifs are the little pieces attached to the end of each stroke of the letter.) However, for a sans serif typeface (one without serifs), it is sometimes sufficient to simply slant the shapes by 15 degrees or so. This can be done automatically by the computer so the typeface designer need only design the Roman shapes. Unfortunately, automatically producing a Bold face from a Roman one is rather more difficult, so it is usually done manually, albeit with help of computer tools. Figure 9.14 shows an automatically generated oblique face and a separately designed italic face.

The full 1,328 glyphs of the Palatino Roman typeface are displayed in appendix D. Can you work out what each group of glyphs is used for?

Oblique Italic

Oblique Italic

Figure 9.14   Oblique and Italic shapes

Problems

For solutions, see appendix B.

The following words have been badly spaced. Photocopy or print this page, cut out the letters, and then paste them onto another page along a straight line, finding an arrangement that is neither too tight nor too loose.

1   P a l a t i n o

2   A V E R S I O N

3   *C o n j e c t u r e*

Summary

- Typefaces can be surprisingly complex, accounting for elements such as accents, alternative glyphs, small caps, and symbols.
- Characters are picked and placed next to each other to form words and lines using bounding boxes and other metrics.
- Typefaces for Eastern alphabets and writing systems can be even more complex.

Words to paragraphs 10

This chapter covers

- Splitting paragraphs into lines with spacing and hyphenation
- Splitting paragraphs over pages
- Setting type before the computer age

We have learned how to design individual characters of a typeface using lines and curves and how to combine these characters into words and sentences. Now we must combine the words and sentences into paragraphs and the paragraphs into pages. This will involve choosing how to space and where to break the lines and paragraphs even if they do not fit conveniently. It is, like many things in book layout, a combination of calculation and taste.

10.1 A paragraph of text

Look at the two paragraphs from Franz Kafka's *Metamorphosis* shown in figure 10.1. What do we notice? The left- and right-hand sides of the block of text are straight—no ragged edges. This is called *full justification*. We notice that some of the lines have a hyphen at the end, in the middle of a word. Looking carefully, we see that the spacing between words is not consistent from line to line. The last line of each paragraph does not go all the way to the end; the first may be indented.

One morning, when Gregor Samsa woke from troubled dreams, he found himself transformed in his bed into a horrible vermin. He lay on his armour-like back, and if he lifted his head a little he could see his brown belly, slightly domed and divided by arches into stiff sections. The bedding was hardly able to cover it and seemed ready to slide off any moment. His many legs, pitifully thin compared with the size of the rest of him, waved about helplessly as he looked.

"What's happened to me?" he thought. It wasn't a dream. His room, a proper human room although a little too small, lay peacefully between its four familiar walls. A collection of textile samples lay spread out on the table – Samsa was a travelling salesman – and above it there hung a picture that he had recently cut out of an illustrated magazine and housed in a nice, gilded frame. It showed a lady fitted out with a fur hat and fur boa who sat upright, raising a heavy fur muff that covered the whole of her lower arm towards the viewer.

Figure 10.1   Our example text from Kafka's Metamorphosis

How do we build a line or paragraph from a list of letters? We know that each letter in a typeface has an origin as well as an advancement that specifies how far to move to the right after drawing a character. We also know about kerning, which tells us that certain letter combinations must appear closer together. Figure 10.2 shows a line of text with the (usually invisible) boxes that help to position each character.

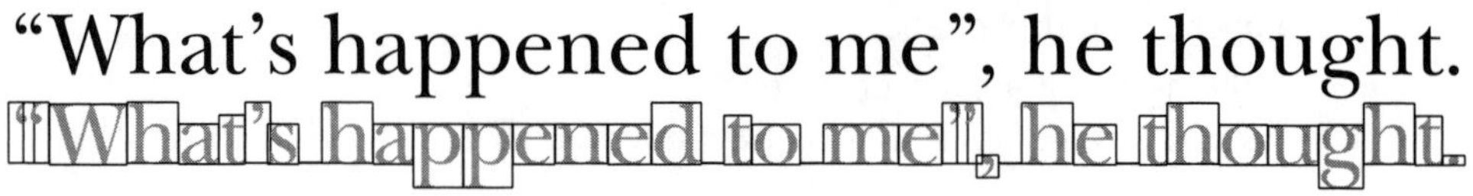

"What's happened to me", he thought.

Figure 10.2   Boxes help to position characters.

If all our characters fortuitously added up to the correct width for a line, or we were happy to break ords with hyphens anywhere, or we did not want a straight right edge, this is all we would have to do. We would draw the characters in order until we reached the end of a line and then start on the next line, moving down the page the right amount (called the *leading*—pronounced "ledding"). Alas, the world is not that simple, and we must add space to fill out the line. This can look poor if done badly, especially when a narrow column is used, such as in a newspaper. Figure 10.3 shows an example of poor full justification.

F   u   l   l justification in a   narrow column   can make big gaps between words and letters.

Figure 10.3   Full justification can be ugly.

Here, space has been added not only between words but also between letters to make the line fit. Generally, we like to add most of the needed space between words, rather than between individual letters. Figure 10.4 shows a paragraph typeset to three different column widths.

Notice how the result improves as the column becomes wider; fewer compromises have to be made. In fact, no hyphens at all are required in the widest case. In the narrowest column, we refuse to add extra space between the letters of the compound word *armour-like* but choose rather to produce an under-full line in this case. This decision is a matter of taste, of course. Another option is to give up on the idea of straight left and right edges and set the text as *ragged right*. The idea is to make no

One morning,
when Gregor
Samsa woke
from troubled
dreams, he
found himself
transformed in
his bed into a
horrible vermin.
He lay on his
armour-like
back, and if
he…

One morning, when
Gregor Samsa woke
from troubled dreams,
he found himself trans-
formed in his bed into
a horrible vermin. He
lay on his armour-like
back, and if he lifted his
head a little he could see
his brown belly, slightly
domed and divided by
arches into stiff sections.

One morning, when Gregor
Samsa woke from troubled
dreams, he found himself
transformed in his bed into a
horrible vermin. He lay on his
armour-like back, and if he lifted
his head a little he could see
his brown belly, slightly domed
and divided by arches into stiff
sections.

Figure 10.4   Full justification with different column widths

changes in the spacing of words at all, just ending a line when the next word will not fit.
This also eliminates hyphenation. Figure 10.5 is a paragraph set first ragged right and
and then fully justified.

One morning, when
Gregor Samsa woke from
troubled dreams, he found
himself transformed in his
bed into a horrible vermin.
He lay on his armour-like
back, and if he lifted his
head a little he could see
his brown belly, slightly
domed and divided by
arches into stiff sections.

One morning, when Gre-
gor Samsa woke from trou-
bled dreams, he found himself transformed in his bed
into a horrible vermin. He
lay on his armour-like back,
and if he lifted his head a little he could see his brown
belly, slightly domed and
divided by arches into stiff
sections.

Figure 10.5   Ragged right and full justification

10.2 *Hyphenation*

If we decide we must hyphenate a word because we cannot stretch or shrink a line without
making it too ugly, how do we choose where to break it? We could just hyphenate as
soon as the line is full, irrespective of where we are in the word. In figure 10.6, the
paragraph on the left prefers hyphenation at any point to adding or removing space
between words. The paragraph on the right follows usual typesetting and hyphenation
rules, preferring the adding of space to hyphenation.

These are very ugly hyphenations, however: we have *trouble-d, o-n,* and *h-e.* Every word
has places that are better or worse for hyphenation. We would prefer *trou-bled* and
on. Some words must be hyphenated differently depending on context: for example,
rec-ord for the noun and *re-cord* for the verb. In addition, authorities on hyphenation
(such as dictionaries, which include hyphenation information) do not always agree:

One morning, when Grego- r Samsa woke from trouble- d dreams, he found himself transformed in his bed into a horrible vermin. He lay o- n his armour-like back, and if he lifted his head a little h- e could see his brown belly, slightly domed and divided by arches into stiff sections.	One morning, when Gregor Samsa woke from troubled dreams, he found himself transformed in his bed into a horrible vermin. He lay on his armour-like back, and if he lifted his head a little he could see his brown belly, slightly domed and divided by arches into stiff sections.

Figure 10.6   Hyphenation by preference (left) and spacing by preference (right)

Webster's Dictionary has *in-de-pen-dent* and *tri-bune*, and *American Heritage Dictionary* has *in-de-pend-ent* and *trib-une*. There are also words that should never be hyphenated. For example, there is no really good place to break *squirm*.

There are two methods for solving this problem automatically as the computer typesets the lines: a *dictionary-based* system simply stores an entire word list with the hyphenation points for each word. This method ensures perfect hyphenation for known words but does not help us at all when a new word is encountered (as it often is in scientific or technical publications or if we need to hyphenate a proper noun, such as a the name of a person or city). The alternative is a *rule-based* system, which follows a set of rules about what are typically good and bad breaks. For example, "a break is always allowable after *q* if followed by a vowel," "a hyphen is fine before *-ness*," or "a hyphen is good between *x* and *p* in all circumstances." We may also have *inhibiting* rules, such as "never break *b-ly*." Some patterns may only apply at the beginning or end of a word; others apply anywhere. In fact, these rules can be derived automatically from a list of the correct hyphenations and be expected to work well for other unknown words (assuming those words are in the same language; we require a hyphenation dictionary for each language appearing in the document). For example, in the typesetting system used for this book, there are 8,527 rules and only 8 exceptional cases that must be listed explicitly, as shown in figure 10.7.

```
uni-ver-sity        ma-nu-scripts
uni-ver-sit-ies     re-ci-pro-city
how-ever            through-out
ma-nu-script        some-thing
```

Figure 10.7   Special cases in hyphenation

Thus far, we have assumed that decisions on hyphenation are made once we reach the end of a line and find we are about to overrun it. If we are, we alter the spacing between words, hyphenate, or some combination of the two. And so, at most we need to re-typeset the current line. Advanced line-breaking algorithms use a more complicated approach, seeking to optimize the result for a whole paragraph. (We have gone line-by-line, making the best line we can for the first line, then the second, etc.) It may turn out that an awkward situation later in the paragraph is prevented by making a slightly less-than-optimal decision in an earlier line, such as squeezing in an extra word or hyphenating in a good position when not strictly required. We can assign *demerits* to certain situations (a hyphenation, too much or too little spacing between words, and so on) and optimize the outcome for the least sum of such demerits. These sorts of optimization algorithms can be quite slow for large paragraphs, taking an amount of time equal to the square of the number of lines in the paragraph. For normal texts, this additional time is not a problem since we are unlikely to have more than a few 10s of lines in a single paragraph.

10.3 Paragraphs on a page

We have now dealt with splitting a text into lines and paragraphs; let's look at similar problems that occurs when it comes to fitting those paragraphs onto a page. There are two worrying situations: when the last line of a paragraph is *widowed* at the top of the next page and when the first line of a paragraph is *orphaned* on the last line of a page. Examples of a widow and an orphan are shown in figure 10.8.

Figure 10.8 A widow (top) and orphan (bottom).

It is difficult to deal with these problems without upsetting the balance of the whole two-page spread, but it can be done by slightly increasing or decreasing line spacing on one side. Another option, of course, is to edit the text, and you may be surprised to learn how often that happens.

Further small adjustments and improvements to reduce the amount of hyphenation can be introduced using *microtypography*. Microtypography involves stretching or shrinking the individual characters in a line horizontally, hoping to make the line fit without the need for hyphenation. Of course, if taken to extremes, this would remove all hyphens but make the page unreadable! Shrinking or stretching by up to 2% seems to be hard to notice, though.

Another way to improve the look of a paragraph is to allow punctuation to hang over the end of the line. For example, a comma or a hyphen should hang a little over the right-hand side, which makes the block of the paragraph seem visually more straight even though really we have made it less straight. Figure 10.9 shows a narrow paragraph without (left) and with (middle) overhanging punctuation. The vertical line (right) highlights the overhanging hyphens and commas used to keep the right-hand margin visually straight.

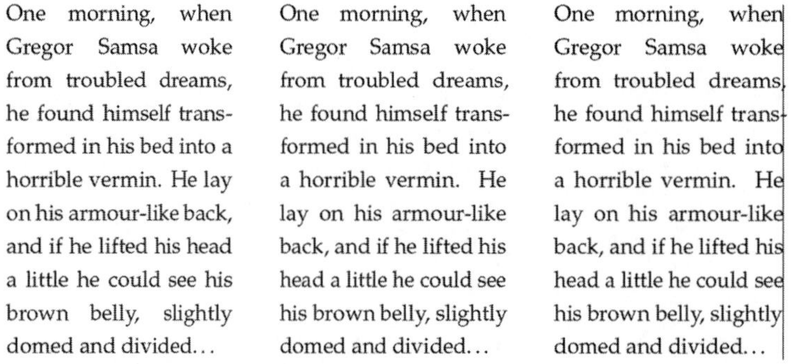

One morning, when Gregor Samsa woke from troubled dreams, he found himself trans-formed in his bed into a horrible vermin. He lay on his armour-like back, and if he lifted his head a little he could see his brown belly, slightly domed and divided...

One morning, when Gregor Samsa woke from troubled dreams, he found himself trans-formed in his bed into a horrible vermin. He lay on his armour-like back, and if he lifted his head a little he could see his brown belly, slightly domed and divided...

One morning, when Gregor Samsa woke from troubled dreams, he found himself trans-formed in his bed into a horrible vermin. He lay on his armour-like back, and if he lifted his head a little he could see his brown belly, slightly domed and divided...

Figure 10.9   **A paragraph with (left) and without (center and right) overhanging punctuation**

A further distracting visual problem in paragraphs is that of *rivers*. These are the vertical lines of white space that occur when spaces on successive lines are in just the wrong place, as shown in figure 10.10.

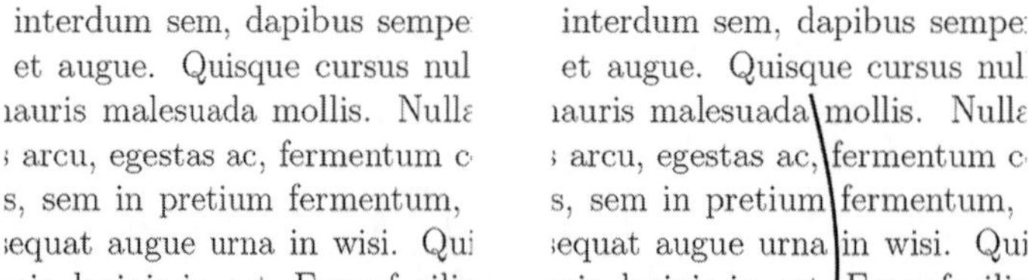

interdum sem, dapibus sempe
et augue. Quisque cursus nul
iauris malesuada mollis. Nulla
; arcu, egestas ac, fermentum c
s, sem in pretium fermentum,
;equat augue urna in wisi. Qui
juis, lacinia in, est. Fusce facilis

interdum sem, dapibus sempe
et augue. Quisque cursus nul
iauris malesuada mollis. Nulla
; arcu, egestas ac, fermentum c
s, sem in pretium fermentum,
;equat augue urna in wisi. Qui
juis, lacinia in, est. Fusce facilis

Figure 10.10   **A river in a paragraph**

We have shown the river with a line. Notice that the word *fermentum*, which appears in almost the same place on two successive lines, is also distracting. The problem is difficult to deal with automatically, and the text may have to be edited to fix it. The previously discussed microtypographical techniques can help a little; since there are fewer widened spaces between words, the rivers will be narrower and less noticeable.

10.4 Before computers

You may wonder how type was set before computers. It was set in much the same way, it turns out, but with many more manual steps and a lot of little pieces of metal. Figure 10.11 shows one such piece, for the character *n* at a particular size, in a particular typeface.

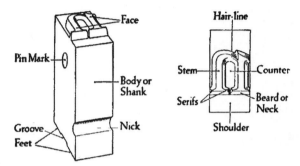

Figure 10.11   A piece of metal type

These pieces of metal are picked from a tray of boxes, by hand, and placed in rows into a *composing stick*: each word is separated by little metal spaces, and each row is spaced by a metal strip (the leading). You can imagine that many, many copies of these little metal pieces were required for each typeface and size so it was an expensive business. Because it will eventually be used for printing by being inked and stamped or rolled on paper, the type is mirrored, and thus hard to read, and one must be careful not to mix up *p* and *q* or *b* and *d*. (This is one possible origin of the phrase "Mind your Ps and Qs.") This painstaking process is shown in figures 10.12 and 10.13.

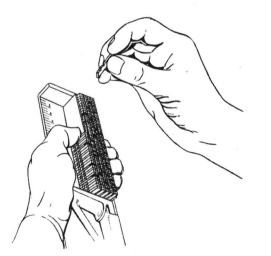

Figure 10.12   A whole paragraph of metal type   **Figure 10.13   The compositor at work**

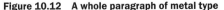

The finished paragraphs of type are arranged in a *galley*. The galley will be used to make prints of the page (or pages—two or four may be printed from one galley and then folded and cut). You can imagine how long it takes to make up the galleys for a book and how much time is required to justify each line by inserting exactly the right spaces and hyphenating by hand. Mistakes found after test prints can be very costly to fix since they necessitate taking apart the galley and replacing not just a single character, but perhaps re-typesetting a whole paragraph. Figure 10.14 shows a galley ready for printing:

Figure 10.14   Pages of set type. (Photo courtesy of Tom Garnett at the Print Shop of the Cambridge Museum of Technology, Cambridge, UK)

Eventually, machines were developed to automatically place the pieces of type based on what was typed on a keyboard and to automatically justify each line. Such mechanical systems were in common use until the advent of *phototypesetting*. Phototypesetting involved building an image by shining light through a series of stencils onto photosensitive paper and then photographing it. Computer typesetting supplanted both of these methods in the late 20th century.

Problems

For solutions, see appendix B.

Identify good hyphenation points in the following words:

1 hyphenation
2 fundraising
3 arithmetic (noun)
4 arithmetic (adjective)
5 demonstration
6 demonstrative

7 genuine

8 mountainous

Summary

- Characters are placed together into words and lines and then into paragraphs and pages.
- Thousands of such tiny shapes can make up a page of text.
- Lines of text can be manipulated by adjusting the space between letters or hyphenating words to change the flow of the text as needed.
- Before computers, typesetting was done by placing tiny metal shapes into a frame by hand.
- Typesetting is now done in the blink of an eye by computer.

11

Out into the world

This chapter covers

- Producing final output for a book
- Print and eBook formats
- What's in a PDF

We have seen how to define shapes for characters and graphics and how arrays of colored pixels are used to represent photographs digitally. We have combined characters into words and those words into paragraphs. But how do we get our creation into the hands of the reader?

If the book is to be printed, we must send it to the printer: What will they require to ensure it looks on the paper just as we see it on the screen? If we are delivering it electronically to the reader as an eBook, how do we produce it in the format required by the eBook reader? In this chapter, we answer these questions.

11.1 Final output for printing

In the previous chapter, we looked at traditional metal typesetting, but let's look nearer to the present day, just before computer publishing as we know it took over in the late 20th century. Figure 11.1 shows a page of adverts being "pasted up" (i.e., pieces of text, line art, and images being glued onto a piece of paper to make the final layout). The individual pieces might have been text printed via other mechanisms,

114

hand-drawn images, or photographs. Images that needed to be made larger or smaller would have been photographically enlarged or shrunk prior to the final paste-up. As you can imagine, the paste-up process was lengthy and error prone.

Figure 11.1   Pasting up a page

Figure 11.2 shows a machine for photographing the pasted-up page onto a photographic negative with an intervening halftone screen to convert the grayscale page to a purely black-and-white one. This negative could then be used to make plates for a variety of physical printing processes. The pasted-up sheet was therefore known as *camera-ready copy*, a phrase that is still sometimes used today to refer to the output of more modern computer typesetting systems, even when cameras are no longer involved.

Figure 11.2   Film camera for photographing pasted-up pages for typesetting

In the 1980s and 1990s, first professionally and then at home, desktop publishing became available and then widespread. The typography, layout, and figures on the computer screen closely resembled the final printed output. Manual paste-up was no longer required. However, the emphasis was still very much on the production of the printed output on a paper. Still more recently, there has been a significant shift from printed books to electronically reproduced ones, read using either a dedicated eBook reader or simply a computer, tablet, or mobile phone screen. Readers of this book, for example, are more likely to be enjoying it in digital than physical form.

11.2   eBooks

The eBook (electronic book) came to prominence in the early 2000s. In its hardware incarnation—for example, the Amazon Kindle illustrated in figure 11.3 or the larger BOOX in figure 11.4—it consists of a low power-consumption black-and-white or grayscale display, together with the memory to hold the text of hundreds of books and the computing power to lay them out on the screen. Such devices have battery lives between recharging measured in weeks, not hours.

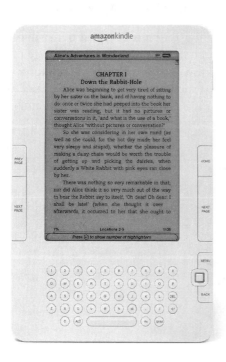

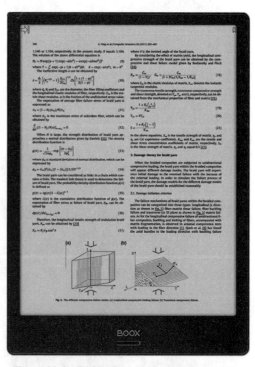

Figure 11.3   An early Kindle eBook reader from Amazon

Figure 11.4   BOOX eBook reader showing a page from a PDF document

There are, broadly, two kinds of eBook reader. Devices intended largely for reading novels or other books with minimal illustration or technical content, like the Amazon Kindle, store their books in a basic markup format, such as the ones we looked at in chapter 3. The user can then adjust the font and font size, and the text will 'reflow' to fill the screen. Similarly, the book can be read on a small or large device at the same font size, just with shorter or longer lines as appropriate. Control of the formatting is shared between the author and the reader.

The other common format for eBooks is Adobe's Portable Document Format, or PDF, with which most of us are familiar. The larger eBook in figure 11.4 is displaying a PDF, which you can see contains formatting, such as equations, that really requires a fixed layout to be maintained. This fixed formatting is, of course, the same requirement we have when putting our book together to be sent, camera-ready, to a printer.

11.3 Introducing PDF

The PDF is a standard way of representing multipage documents containing text, graphics, and images so that they may be printed or electronically transmitted without loss of fidelity. Take, for example, the page from this book reproduced in figure 11.5. It contains text, of course, which is a sequence of glyphs drawn from a font. The font is embedded inside the PDF and so travels with it. The page also contains pixel-based images (top and middle) and a line drawing (bottom). With just these three things—text, pixel images, and line drawings—we can build any page of any book.

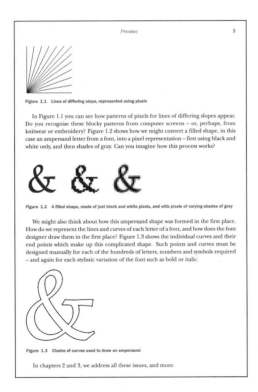

Figure 11.5 A page containing text, images, and a line drawing

A PDF also contains metadata—that is, data about the PDF that is not part of the page itself. For example, many PDFs have an interactive table of contents, which a PDF reader will present at the side of the document. Figure 11.6 shows such a table for this book.

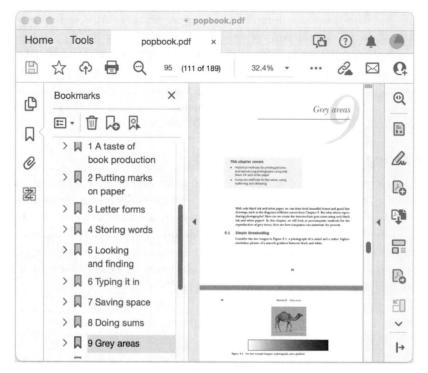

Figure 11.6   A PDF has metadata, too—in this case, an interactive table of contents.

We will now build a very simple PDF from scratch, showing you the gory details of the PDF file format itself. We will not be able to explain every aspect, even in our simple example, but we will discuss as much as we can.

11.4   Building a PDF

We begin by building the page content itself. Then, we will add the rest of the PDF structure around it. The page content is a series of numbers and strings, together with various operators to do different things. The following listing shows the sequence needed to move to a position and write some text.

Listing 11.1   Adding some text

```
1 0 0 1 20 150 cm  ❶     Move to (20, 150)
BT
  /F0 36 Tf  ❷     Set font
  (Hello, World!) Tj  ❸     Draw text
ET
```

First, we use the `cm` (current matrix) operator to move to a given position on the page ❶. The mathematics of matrices is beyond our scope, but the six numbers preceding the `cm` may be used to indicate moving, scaling, rotating, and so on. Next, we start a text section with the `BT` (begin text) operator. We set the font ❷ to 36pt `/F0` (which we will define later) using the `Tf` (text font) operator. We can now draw the text ❸ using the `Tj` operator and, finally, end the text section with `ET` (end text). The result is shown in figure 11.7.

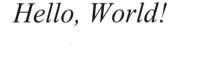

Figure 11.7   Our new PDF with text

Now that we have some text, we will add graphics. In a moment, we will add a very basic pixel-based image, but let's first add a very simple vector graphic: a line to underline our text. Just like the text, this line will scale smoothly to any size in our PDF viewer or to any resolution when the PDF is printed. Our line-drawing commands, which follow our text-drawing commands, are shown in the following listing.

Listing 11.2   Underlining our text

```
0 -3 m    ❶    Move to (0, -3)
80 -3 l   ❷    Draw to (80, -3)
S  ❸   Stroke
88 -3 m
200 -3 l
S
```

To underline the text, we need two lines (because the comma dips below the baseline of the text). We are already positioned at the beginning of the baseline of the text thanks to the positioning command we already used to place the text. So, we move ❶ down a little, add a line up to the comma ❷, and then ask the PDF reader to *stroke* the line ❸ (i.e., actually draw it). This procedure is repeated for the other half of the underlining. The result of adding these underlining operations is shown in figure 11.8.

Finally, we will add a simple image. It is difficult to show the data for a large image in a book like this, so we will make a tiny one of just 5 by 5 pixels, a gray gradient, and then display it scaled up by 100 times. The code is shown in listing 11.3.

> *Hello, World!*

Figure 11.8   Adding underlining with drawing commands

Listing 11.3   Adding an image

```
q ❶     Save state
(all our graphics code so far)
Q ❷     Restore state
100 0 0 100 20 20 cm ❸     Position and scale
BI
/W 5 ❹     Image information (width etc.)
/H 5
/CS /G
/BPC 8
/F /AHx
ID
DD DD DD DD DD ❺     Image data
BB BB BB BB BB
99 99 99 99 99
77 77 77 77 77
55 55 55 55 55 >
EI
```

Our original series of operators is bookended by a q/Q pair ❶❷, which saves the position. Now, the position is back to default, and we can use another cm operator ❸ to position our image at (20, 20) and scale it by 100 times. Then, a flurry of operators include the image information ❹ and the image data itself ❺, which you are not expected to understand. The result is shown in figure 11.9.

Figure 11.9   A pixel-based image is added.

Now that we have completed the page description, we must place it in a PDF object, along with several others, together with a top and a tail to make a valid PDF. You can see our final PDF in the following listing.

Listing 11.4 Our PDF skeleton

```
1 0 obj ❶     Page tree
«/Type /Pages /Kids [3 0 R] /Count 1»
endobj
2 0 obj ❷     Page description
«/Length 235»
stream
(all of our page data from above)
endstream
endobj
3 0 obj ❸     Page
«/Type /Page
  /Parent 1 0 R
  /Resources
    «/Font
      «/F0 «/Type /Font /Subtype /Type1 /BaseFont /Times-Italic»»
    »
  /MediaBox[0 0 300 200]
  /Rotate 0
  /Contents[2 0 R]
»
endobj
4 0 obj ❹     Root object
«/Type /Catalog /Pages 1 0 R»
endobj
xref
0 5 ❺     PDF trailer
0000000000 65535 f
0000000015 00000 n
0000000066 00000 n
0000000163 00000 n
0000000348 00000 n
trailer
«/Root 4 0 R /Size 5»
startxref
393
```

Our PDF begins with the header %PDF-1.1 (PDF version 1.1). It then has four objects. The first, object 1 ❶ (marked 1 0 obj), is the *page tree*. In our case, it consists of only one page, which we can see from the reference 3 0 R is stored in object 3. The next object is the page contents ❷ itself, the sequence of operators we have already written. The next object is the page object ❸, which links to the page contents we have already seen. It also defines our font and the size of the page (300 by 200). The final object ❹ is the document catalog, which is the place where a PDF reader starts when reading the file.

After our objects is the PDF trailer ❺, the details of which we will not discuss. Now, when Adobe Reader, or any other PDF reader, sees this file, it interprets it as a PDF and displays the rendered page, as shown in figure 11.10.

Figure 11.10   Our PDF file in Adobe Reader

The PDF reader can find the font because it is one of a tiny number of standard fonts that every PDF reader has access to. In the vast majority of real PDFs, the fonts are, in fact, embedded in the file, which is why we can view a PDF on any device. This is not true of, for example, files produced by a word processor like Microsoft Word: if you send a Word file to a friend and use a font they do not have on their machine, it will be substituted for another, and the page will look different.

We can see that the PDF format used for an eBook is very much like a printed book: it replicates the layout of the page entirely. As we have seen, an alternative method, best used for books that are mostly or all text such as novels, is embodied by eBook devices, such as the Amazon Kindle. The content is laid out in the right size for whatever device is being used, and the text reflows if the user chooses to change the font size, rotate the device to landscape, or change devices. But for a book like this one with lots of drawings and images, where the layout is very important, PDF is the better choice for most readers.

Conclusion

We now have everything to make a book. We began from scratch, by considering how to place dots of black ink on the white page. Then we learned about shapes and letters, images, paragraphs, and pages. Along the way, we looked at some of the history of book production and took detours into computation, keyboards, and engravings.

Now that you have learned about these topics, you may find you can spot many of the things described in this book. You might see a bad kern or a poorly laid-out paragraph, a pixelated line, a halftone pattern on an advertising hoarding, or a foreign-language keyboard on holiday. Perhaps you might even start work on your own book!

Summary

- Computers have taken away much of the drudgery of book publishing.
- Print publication and eBook publication have differing requirements in page layout, format, and text reflowability.
- We can put together all our text and graphics into a single format, the PDF, suitable both for print and electronic publication.
- For eBooks requiring reflowable text and with few graphics, specific eBook device formats are preferred to PDF.

appendix A
Further reading

A list of interesting books for each chapter follows. Some are closely related to the chapter contents, and some, tangentially. The level of expertise required to understand each of them varies quite a bit, but do not be afraid to read books you do not understand all of, especially if you can obtain or borrow them at little cost.

Chapter 1

Berry, John D., and Roger Black. *Contemporary Newspaper Design: Shaping the News in the Digital Age—Typography & Image on Modern Newsprint.* Mark Batty, 2007. ISBN 0972424032.

Foley, James D., Andries van Dam, Steven K. Fiener, and John F. Hughes. *Computer Graphics: Principles and Practice.* 2nd ed. Addison Wesley, 1995. ISBN 0201848406.

Chapter 2

Lockwood, E.H. *A Book of Curves.* Cambridge University Press, 1961. ISBN 0521044448.

Lupton, Ellen. *Thinking with Type: A Critical Guide for Designers, Writers, Editors, and Students.* 2nd ed. Princeton Architectural Press, 2010. ISBN 1568989695.

Waters, John L. *Fifty Typefaces That Changed the World: Design Museum Fifty.* Conran, 2013. ISBN 184091629X.

Chapter 3

Chadwick, John. *The Decipherment of Linear B.* 2nd ed. Cambridge University Press, 1967. ISBN 1107691761.

Petzold, Charles. *Code: The Hidden Language of Computer Hardware and Software.* Microsoft Press, 2000. ISBN 0735611319.

Polybius. *The Histories.* Robin Waterfield, trans. Oxford University Press/Oxford World Classics, 2010. ISBN 0199534705.

Korpela, Jukka K. *Unicode Explained.* O'Reilly Media, 2006. ISBN 059610121X.

Chapter 4

Cormen, T., C. Leiserson, R. Rivest, and C. Stein. *Introduction to Algorithms.* 3rd ed. MIT Press, 2009. ISBN 0262533057.

Langville, Amy N., and Carl D. Meyer. *Google's PageRank and Beyond: The Science of Search Engine Rankings.* Princeton University Press, 2012. ISBN 0691152667.

Navarro, Gonzalo, and Mathieu Raffinot. *Flexible Pattern Matching in Strings: Practical On-Line Search Algorithms for Texts and Biological Sequences.* Cambridge University Press, 2007. ISBN 0521039932.

Chapter 5

Bliven, Bruce, Jr. *The Wonderful Writing Machine.* Random House, 1954. ISBN 600150329X.

Lundmark, Torbjörn. *Quirky Qwerty: The Story of the Keyboard @ Your Fingertips.* University of New South Wales Press, 2001. ISBN 0868404365.

Wershler-Henry, Darren. *The Iron Whim: A Fragmented History of Typewriting.* McClelland & Stewart, 2005. ISBN 0771089252.

Chapter 6

Margolis, Andrew. *The Fax Modem Sourcebook.* Wiley, 1995. ISBN 0471950726.

Pu, Ida Mengyi. *Fundamental Data Compression.* Butterworth-Heinemann, 2006. ISBN 0750663103.

Sayood, Khalid. *Introduction to Data Compression.* 4th ed. The Morgan Kaufmann Series in Multimedia Information and Systems. Morgan Kaufmann, 2012. ISBN 0124157963.

Chapter 7

Dawson, Mike. *Python Programming for the Absolute Beginner.* 3rd ed. Course Technology PTR, 2010. ISBN 1435455002.

Tate, Bruce A. *Seven Languages in Seven Weeks: A Pragmatic Guide to Learning Programming Languages.* Pragmatic Bookshelf, 2010. ISBN 193435659X.

Whitington, John. *OCaml from the Very Beginning.* Coherent Press, 2013. ISBN 0957671105.

Chapter 8

Gascgoine, Bamber. *How to Identify Prints.* 2nd ed. Thames & Hudson, 2004. ISBN 0500284806.

Griffiths, Antony. *Prints and Printmaking: An Introduction to the History and Techniques.* University of California Press, 1996. ISBN 0520207149.

Hind, Arthur M. *A History of Engraving and Etching.* Dover Publications, 1963. ISBN 0486209547.

Ulichney, Robert. *Digital Halftoning.* The MIT Press, 1987. ISBN 0262210096.

Chapter 9

Bringhurst, Robert. *The Elements of Typographic Style.* Hartley & Marks, 2004. ISBN 0881792065.

Coles, Stephen. *The Geometry of Type: The Anatomy of 100 Essential Typefaces.* Thames and Hudson, 2013. ISBN 0500241422.

Garfield, Simon. *Just My Type: A Book About Fonts.* Profile Books, 2011. ISBN 1846683025.

Chapter 10

Knuth, Donald E. *Digital Typography.* CSLI Lecture Notes, No. 78. Center for the Study of Language and Information (Stanford, California), 1999. ISBN 1575860104.

Slinn, Judith, Sebastian Carter, and Richard Southall. *History of the Monotype Corporation.* Andrew Boag and Christopher Burke, eds. Vanbrugh Press, 2014. ISBN 0993051005.

Southall, Richard. *Printer's Type in the Twentieth Century: Manufacturing and Design Methods.* Oak Knoll Press, 2005. ISBN 1584561552.

Thành, Hàn Thê . *Micro-Typographic Extensions to the TEX Typesetting System.* PhD Dissertation, Masaryk University, Brno, October 2000.

Chapter 11

International Organization for Standardization. *ISO 32000-2: Document Management—Portable Document Format.* ISO 32000-2:2020(E). ISO, 2020.

Whitington, John. *PDF Explained.* O'Reilly, 2012. ISBN 1449310028.

appendix B
Solutions

Chapter 1

1

For the diamond, if we start on the left hand side, we have (2, 10)—(10, 18)—(18, 10)—(10, 2)—(2, 10). For the star, if we start at the bottom left point, we have (3, 3)—(10, 19)—(17, 3)—(1, 13)—(19, 13)—(3, 3).

2

We see a crude representation of the letter E and the Maltese cross.

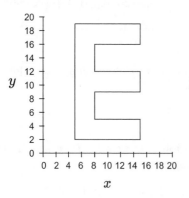
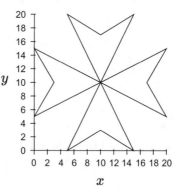

3

For example:

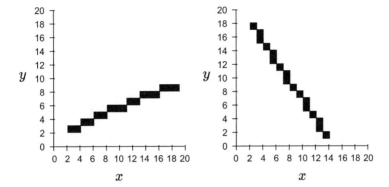

4

For example:

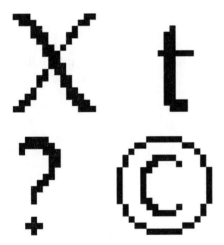

Chapter 2

1

We assign the letters ABCD as in the chapter text:

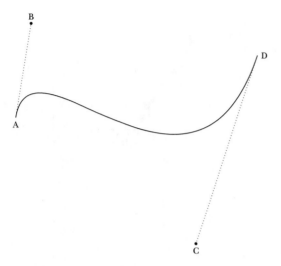

Now, we continue the construction as before, making sure we are not confused by the fact that the line BC now crosses the curve:

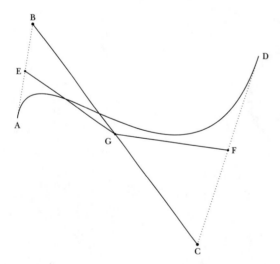

Finally, we finish the construction all the way to J, so our diagram looks like this:

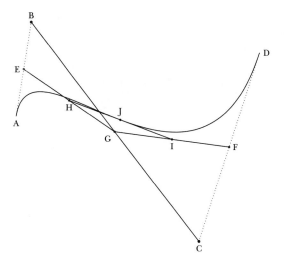

So we have the new Bézier curves AEHJ and JIFD as before:

3

With the even–odd rule:

With the nonzero rule:

Chapter 3

1

32-11-42-54-23-11-14-11-31-24-44-44-31-15-31-11-32-12. There are 18 characters in the message and so 36 numbers to transmit (although in Polybius's system of torches, these would be done two at a time, so just 18 distinct actions). We might use Z for the space character since it doesn't appear often in normal text. We could use ZZZ for end of message.

2

We have 32 rows:

Bits	Number	Letter	Bits	Number	Letter
00000	0	A	10000	16	Q
00001	1	B	10001	17	R
00010	2	C	10010	18	S
00011	3	D	10011	19	T
00100	4	E	10100	20	U
00101	5	F	10101	21	V
00110	6	G	10110	22	W
00111	7	H	10111	23	X
01000	8	I	11000	24	Y
01001	9	J	11001	25	Z
01010	10	K	11010	26	space
01011	11	L	11011	27	.
01100	12	M	11100	28	,
01101	13	N	11101	29	:
01110	14	O	11110	30	;
01111	15	P	11111	31	?

Here, we choose the capital letters and the punctuation *space* . , : ; ? and hope this covers most useful messages.

3

Treason is very much a matter of habit, Smiley decided.

4

84 104 101 109 111 114 101 105 100 101 110 116 105 116 105 101 115 97 109 97 110 104 97 115 44 116 104 101 109 111 114 101 116 104 101 121 101 120 112 114 101 115 115 116 104 101 112 101 114 115 111 110 116 104 101 121 99 111 110 99 101 97 108 46

5

(a) The love of money is the root of *all* evil.

(b) The love of \$\$\$ is the root of all evil.

(c) The love of $\$\$\$$ is the root of all evil.

(d) The love of *\$$\$$\$* is the root of all evil.

Chapter 4

1

(a) The pattern does not match.

(b) The pattern matches at position 17.

(c) The pattern matches at positions 28 and 35.

(d) The pattern matches at position 24.

2

(a) The texts aa, aaa, and aaa, etc. match.

(b) The texts ac and abc only match.

(c) The texts ac, abc, and abbc, etc. match.

(d) The texts ad, abd, acd, abbd, accd, abcd, acbd, abbbd, etc. match.

3

(a) The pattern matches at positions 16 and 17.

(b) The pattern matches at positions 0 and 24.

(c) The pattern matches at positions 0, 1, 24, and 25.

(d) The pattern matches at postiions 0, 1, 24, and 25.

Chapter 6

1

Letter	Frequency	Code	Letter	Frequency	Code
space	41	111	u	5	110100
e	18	100	v	4	110011
o	14	1011	w	4	110010
t	14	0111	f	4	110001
a	13	0110	'	4	010111
h	12	0100	y	3	010101
r	11	0011	.	3	01010000
n	11	0010	,	3	01010001
s	10	0000	p	2	01010010
i	9	11011	l	2	01010011
c	8	10101	q	1	01011000
m	6	10100	E	1	01011001
l	6	00011	S	1	01011010
g	6	110101	T	1	01011011

So we have:

```
'    I            h    a    v    e         a
010111 01010011 111 0100 0110 110011 100 111 0110 111
t      h    e    o    r    y         w    h    i
0111 0100 100 1011 0011 010101 111 110010 0100 11011
c      h         I              s         u         p
10101 0100 111 01010011 111 0000 110100 0000 01010010
e    c    t         i    s         r    a    t    h
100 10101 0111 111 11011 0000 111 0011 0110 0111 0100
e    r    i    m    m    o    r    a    l
100 0011 111 11011 10100 10100 1011 0011 0110 00011
,         '         S    m    i    l    e    y
01010001 010111 111 01011010 10100 11011 00011 100 010101
w    e    n    t         o    n    ,
111 110010 100 0010 0111 111 1011 0010 01010001 111
m    o    r    e    l    i    g    h    t
10100 1011 0011 100 111 00011 11011 110101 0100 0111
l    y         .
00011 010101 01010000
```

2

There are moments that are made up of too much stuff for them to be lived at the time they occur.

3

The lengths and colors are:

Color	Length	Code	Color	Length	Code	Color	Length	Code
White	37	00010110	White	3	1000	White	6	1110
White	5	1100	Black	2	11	Black	2	11
Black	2	11	White	2	0111	White	1	0000111
White	7	1111	Black	2	11	White	1	0000111
Black	7	00011	White	4	1011	Black	2	11
White	7	1111	Black	9	000100	White	6	1110
Black	6	0010	White	3	1000	Black	2	11
White	3	1000	Black	2	11	White	2	0111
White	4	1011	White	10	00111	Black	2	11
Black	4	011	White	2	0111	White	6	1110
White	5	1100	Black	3	10	Black	2	11
Black	9	000100	White	2	0111	White	3	1000
White	4	1011	Black	3	10	Black	2	11
Black	9	000100	White	3	1000	White	5	1100
White	2	0111	Black	9	000100	Black	3	10
White	4	1011	White	3	1000	White	1	0000111
Black	4	011	Black	2	11	White	1	0000111
White	5	1100	White	10	00111	Black	2	11
Black	2	11	White	2	0111	White	6	1110
White	5	1100	Black	8	000101	Black	3	10
Black	3	10	White	3	1000	White	1	0000111
White	3	1000	Black	2	11	Black	10	0000100
Black	2	11	White	5	1100	White	3	1000
White	5	1100	Black	3	10	Black	9	000100
Black	3	10	White	2	0111	White	2	0111
White	1	0000111	Black	2	11	Black	2	11

Color	Length	Code	Color	Length	Code	Color	Length	Code
White	4	1011	White	10	00111	White	8	1011
Black	5	0011	White	2	0111	Black	2	11
White	4	1011	Black	8	000101	White	2	0111
Black	2	11	White	3	1000	Black	7	00011
White	6	1110	Black	2	11	White	6	1110
Black	2	11	White	6	1110	Black	7	00011
White	2	0111	Black	2	11	White	3	1000
Black	2	11	White	2	0111	White	37	00010110
White	7	1111	Black	2	11			
Black	2	11	White	7	1111			
White	1	0000111	Black	2	11			
White	3	1000	White	1	0000111			
Black	2	11	White	1	0000111			
White	2	0111	Black	3	10			
Black	2	11	White	4	1011			
White	4	1011	Black	3	10			
Black	2	11	White	2	0111			
White	5	1100	Black	2	11			
Black	3	10	White	6	1110			
White	2	0111	Black	2	11			
Black	2	11	White	2	0111			
White	10	00111	Black	3	10			

So we have the following:

```
000101101100111110001111100101000101101111 0000010
010110001000111101101111001110010100011110 0110000 1
111011001110111111011011111111110000111100 0110111
010101111100100111110011110001101111110110 00100100
011001110111100111010000001001000110011101 11000101
100011111011011111111110000111000011110101 11010111
111101110001111101100001110000111111101101 10111111110
111000111100100000111000011111111010000011 100001011
000000100011111101111011100011111000010110 00000 1011
0
```

4

The codes are as follows:

Code	Length	Color	Code	Length	Color	Code	Length	Color
00010110	37	White	10	3	Black	10	3	Black
0000111	1	White	0000111	1	White	0111	2	White
00011	7	Black	000100	9	Black	11	2	Black
1111	7	White	1000	3	White	1110	6	White
00011	7	Black	11	2	Black	11	2	Black
1100	5	White	1011	8	White	0000111	1	White
00011	7	Black	11	2	Black	11	2	Black
1000	3	White	0111	2	White	1110	6	White

Code	Length	Color	Code	Length	Color	Code	Length	Color
000100	9	Black	000100	9	Black	11	2	Black
1011	4	White	0111	2	White	0111	2	White
0000100	10	Black	000100	9	Black	011	4	Black
1000	3	White	1000	3	White	1100	5	White
000100	9	Black	11	2	Black	11	2	Black
0111	2	White	1011	8	White	1000	3	White
11	2	Black	11	2	Black	11	2	Black
1100	5	White	0111	2	White	1110	6	White
10	3	Black	000100	9	Black	11	2	Black
1000	3	White	0111	2	White	0000111	1	White
10	3	Black	11	2	Black	0000100	10	Black
1100	5	White	1100	5	White	1000	3	White
10	3	Black	10	3	Black	0000100	10	Black
0111	2	White	0111	2	White	1000	3	White
11	2	Black	11	2	Black	000100	9	Black
1100	5	White	1011	8	White	0111	2	White
10	3	Black	11	2	Black	0000111	1	White
0000111	1	White	0111	2	White	00011	7	Black
11	2	Black	11	2	Black	1111	7	White
1110	6	White	1100	5	White	0010	6	Black
11	2	Black	10	3	Black	1110	6	White
0111	2	White	0000111	1	White	0010	6	Black
10	3	Black	11	2	Black	1011	4	White
1111	7	White	1110	6	White	00010110	37	White
11	2	Black	11	2	Black			
0111	2	White	0111	2	White			
11	2	Black	11	2	Black			
1110	6	White	1011	8	White			
11	2	Black	11	2	Black			
0000111	1	White	0111	2	White			
11	2	Black	11	2	Black			
1100	5	White	1110	6	White			
10	3	Black	11	2	Black			
0111	2	White	0000111	1	White			
11	2	Black	11	2	Black			
1011	8	White	1110	6	White			
11	2	Black	11	2	Black			
0111	2	White	0111	2	White			
11	2	Black	10	3	Black			
1100	5	White	1110	6	White			

So, we have the image:

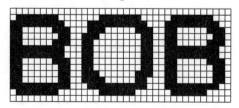

Chapter 7

1

(a)

$$\frac{(1+1)+1}{}$$
$$\Longrightarrow \quad \frac{2+1}{}$$
$$\Longrightarrow \quad 3$$

(b)

$$\frac{(2\times2)\times2}{}$$
$$\Longrightarrow \quad \frac{4\times2}{}$$
$$\Longrightarrow \quad 8$$

(c)

$$\frac{(2\times3)+4}{}$$
$$\Longrightarrow \quad \frac{6+4}{}$$
$$\Longrightarrow \quad 10$$

2

(a)

$$x\times x\times y$$
$$\Longrightarrow \quad \frac{4\times4\times5}{}$$
$$\Longrightarrow \quad \frac{16\times5}{}$$
$$\Longrightarrow \quad 80$$
$$z\times y+z$$
$$\Longrightarrow \quad \frac{100\times5+100}{}$$
$$\Longrightarrow \quad \frac{500+100}{}$$
$$\Longrightarrow \quad 600$$

(b)

$$z\times z$$
$$\Longrightarrow \quad \frac{100\times100}{}$$
$$\Longrightarrow \quad 10000$$

3

(a)

$$
\begin{array}{ll}
& \underline{\text{f } 4\ 5} \\
\Longrightarrow & \underline{4 \times 5} \times 4 \\
\Longrightarrow & \underline{20 \times 4} \\
\Longrightarrow & \underline{80}
\end{array}
$$

(b)

$$
\begin{array}{ll}
& \text{f } \underline{(\text{f } 4\ 5)}\ 5 \\
\Longrightarrow & \underline{\text{f } 80\ 5} \\
\Longrightarrow & \underline{80 \times 5} \times 80 \\
\Longrightarrow & \underline{400 \times 80} \\
\Longrightarrow & 32000
\end{array}
$$

(c)

$$
\begin{array}{ll}
& \text{f } \underline{(\text{f } 4\ 5)}\ \underline{(\text{f } 4\ 5)} \\
\Longrightarrow & \text{f } \underline{80\ 80} \\
\Longrightarrow & \underline{80 \times 80}\ \times 80 \\
\Longrightarrow & \underline{32000 \times 80} \\
\Longrightarrow & 512000
\end{array}
$$

4

(a)

$$
\begin{array}{ll}
& \underline{\text{f } 5\ 4} = \underline{\text{f } 4\ 5} \\
\Longrightarrow & \underline{80 = 80} \\
\Longrightarrow & \textit{true}
\end{array}
$$

(b)

$$
\begin{array}{ll}
& \text{if } \underline{1 = 2} \text{ then 3 else 4} \\
\Longrightarrow & \underline{\text{if } \textit{false} \text{ then 3 else 4}} \\
\Longrightarrow & 4
\end{array}
$$

(c)

$$\text{if (if } 1 = 2 \text{ then } \mathit{false} \text{ else } \mathit{true}) \text{ then 3 else 4}$$
$$\implies \quad \text{if } \mathit{true} \text{ then 3 else 4}$$
$$\implies \quad 3$$

5

(a)

$$\text{head } [2, 3, 4]$$
$$\implies \quad 2$$

(b)

$$\text{tail } [2]$$
$$\implies \quad []$$

(c)

$$\text{head } [2, 3, 4] \bullet [2, 3, 4]$$
$$\implies \quad [2] \bullet [2, 3, 4]$$
$$\implies \quad [2, 2, 3, 4]$$

6

(a) [] (first if)
(b) [1] (second if)
(c) [1, 3] (via 1 • odds [])

Chapter 8

1

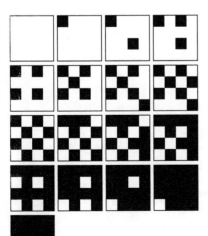

2

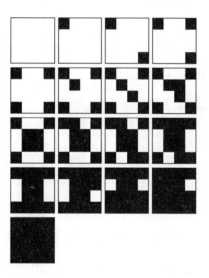

3

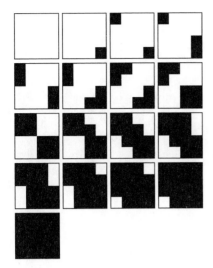

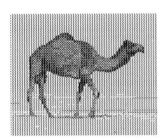

Chapter 9

1

Palatino

2

AVERSION

3

Conjecture

Chapter 10

1

hy-phen-a-tion

2

fund-raising

3

a-rith-me-tic (the noun)

4

ar-ith-me-tic (the adjective)

5

dem-on-stra-tion

6

de-mon-stra-tive

7

gen-u-ine

8

moun-tain-ous

appendix C
Templates

The following pages contain blank templates for answering problems 1.2, 1.3, 1.4, 2.1, 8.1, 8.2, and 8.3.

Problem 1.2

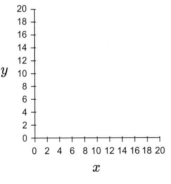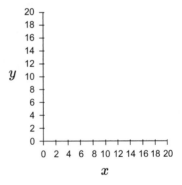

Problem 1.3

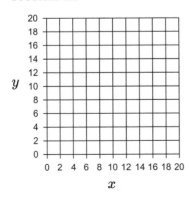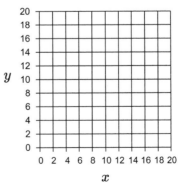

Problem 1.4

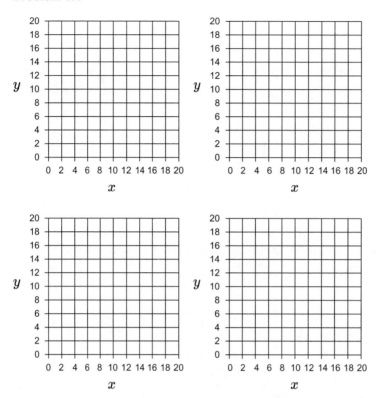

Problem 2.1

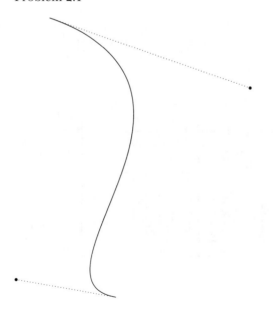

Problem 8.1

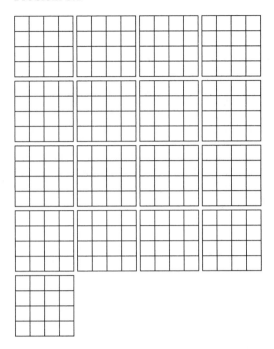

Problem 8.2

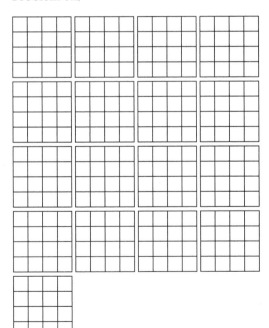

Problem 8.3

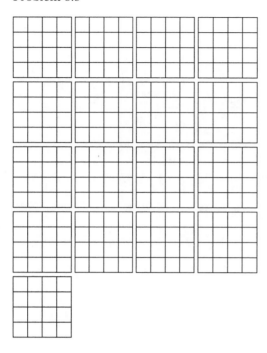

appendix D
Palatino Roman glyphs

@ A B C D E F G H I J K L M N O
P Q R S T U V W X Y Z Á À Â Ä Ã Ă Å
Á̇ Ā Ą Æ Ǽ Ć Ĉ Č Ç Ċ Ď Ð Đ É È Ê Ë Ĕ
Ě Ė Ē Ę Ǵ Ĝ Ğ Ġ Ĥ Ħ Í Ì Î Ï Ĩ Ĭ İ
Ī Į Ĵ Ķ Ḱ Ĺ Ļ Ľ Ļ Ł Ń Ñ Ň Ņ Ṇ Ó Ò
Ô Ö Õ Ǒ Ő Ō Ø Ǿ Œ Ŕ Ř Ŗ Ṛ Ś Ŝ Š Ş Ṣ
Ṭ Ť Ť’ Ţ Ŧ Ú Ù Û Ü Ũ Ŭ Ǔ Ủ Ű Ū Ų Ẃ Ẁ Ŵ
Ẅ Ý Ỳ Ŷ Ÿ Ź Ž Ż Ʒ Ŋ Ŋ Þ a b c d e f
g h i j k l m n o p q r s t u v w x
y z á à â ä ã ă å á̇ ā ą æ ǽ ć ĉ č ç
ċ ď đ é è ê ë ě ĕ ė ē ę ǵ ĝ ğ ǵ ġ ĥ
ħ í ì î ï ĩ ĭ ı ī į ĵ ķ ķ κ ĺ ļ ľ ļ
ŀ ł ń ñ ň ņ ’n ņ ó ò ô ö õ ǒ ő ō ø ǿ
œ ŕ ř ŗ ŗ ś ŝ š ş ş ţ ť ţ ŧ ú ù û ü
ũ ŭ ủ ű ū ų ẃ ẁ ŵ ẅ ý ỳ ŷ ÿ ź ž ż ʒ
ŋ þ ð ß SS IJ Qu Th ch ck ct fi fl ff ffi ffl ft fft
fb ffb fh ffh fk ffk fj ij ſ ſi ſl ſſ ſſi ſſl ſt ſb ſh ſk
ſp ſt tt tz ª º ⁿ a b c d e f g h i j k
l m n o p q r s t u v w x y z æ œ è

0 1 2 3 4 5 6 7 8 9 0 1 2 3 4 5 6 7
8 9 0 1 2 3 4 5 6 7 8 9 0 1 2 3 4 5
6 7 8 9 0 1 2 3 4 5 6 7 8 9 + − = (
) + − = ( ) · , $ ¢ % ‰ ¹/ ½ ⅓ ⅔ ¼ ¾
⅕ ⅖ ⅗ ⅘ ⅙ ⅚ ⅛ ⅜ ⅝ ⅞ $\frac{1}{1}$ $\frac{1}{2}$ $\frac{1}{3}$ $\frac{2}{3}$ $\frac{1}{4}$ $\frac{3}{4}$ $\frac{1}{5}$ $\frac{2}{5}$
$\frac{3}{5}$ $\frac{4}{5}$ $\frac{1}{6}$ $\frac{5}{6}$ $\frac{1}{8}$ $\frac{3}{8}$ $\frac{5}{8}$ $\frac{7}{8}$ + ± − ÷ × = ≠ ≈ < >

Figure D.1   Palatino, glyphs 1–500

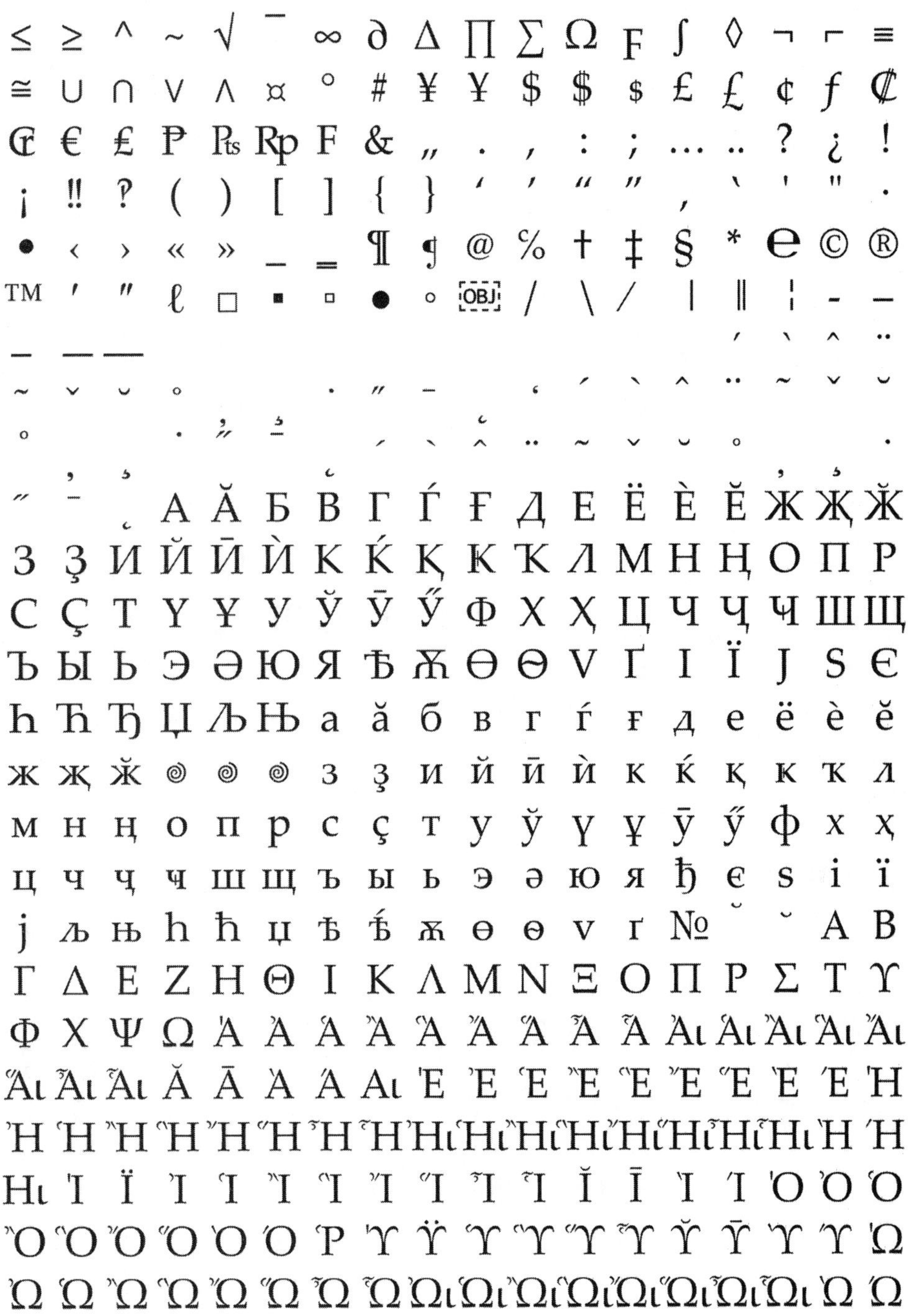

≤ ≥ ^ ~ √ ‾ ∞ ∂ Δ ∏ Σ Ω Ⅎ ∫ ◊ ¬ ⌐ ≡

≅ ∪ ∩ ∨ ∧ ¤ ° # ¥ ¥ $ $ $ £ £ ¢ ƒ ₵

 Є € £ ₧ ₨ Ⅎ & „ . , : ; … ‥ ? ¿ !

¡ ‼ ? ( ) [ ] { } ' ' " " ‚ ' " .

• ‹ › « » _ = ¶ ⁋ @ % † ‡ § * є © ®

™ ′ ″ ℓ □ ∎ ▫ ● ○ [OBJ] / \ ⁄ | ‖ ⁝ - —

‒ — —

~ ˇ ˘ ˚ · ″ ‾ ' ´ ` ^ ˜ ˇ ˘

˚ · ˌ ˍ ´ ` ^ ‥ ˜ ˇ ˘ ˚ ·

˝ ˉ ˳ A Ă Б В Г Ѓ Ғ Д Е Ё Ѐ Ĕ Ж Ӂ Ӂ

З Ӟ И Й Ӣ Ѝ К Ќ Қ Ҡ Л М Н Ң О П Р

С Ҫ Т У Ӯ У Ў Ȳ Ӳ Ф Х Ҳ Ц Ч Ҷ Ӌ Ш Щ

Ъ Ы Ь Э Ә Ю Я Ĕ Ж̄ Ө Ѳ Ѵ Ґ І Ї Ј Ѕ Є

ћ Ђ Ћ Џ Љ Њ а ă б в г ѓ д е ё ѐ ĕ

ж ӂ ӂ ◉ ◎ ◎ з ӟ и й ӣ ѝ к ќ қ ҡ л

м н ң о п р ҫ т у ў ү ұ ȳ ӳ ф х

ц ч ҷ ӌ ш щ ъ ы ь э ә ю я ђ є ѕ і ї

ј љ њ ћ ҳ џ ĕ ĕ ж̄ ө ѳ ѵ ґ № ˘ ˇ A B

Γ Δ E Z H Θ I K Λ M N Ξ O Π P Σ Υ

Φ X Ψ Ω Ἀ Ἁ Ἂ Ἃ Ἄ Ἅ Ἆ Ἇ ᾈ ᾉ ᾊ ᾋ ᾌ

ᾍ ᾎ ᾏ Ᾰ Ᾱ Ὰ Ά ᾼ Ἐ Ἑ Ἒ Ἓ Ἔ Ἕ Ὲ Έ

Ἠ Ἡ Ἢ Ἣ Ἤ Ἥ Ἦ Ἧ ᾘ ᾙ ᾚ ᾛ ᾜ ᾝ ᾞ ᾟ

ᾟ Ἰ Ἱ Ἲ Ἳ Ἴ Ἵ Ἶ Ἷ Ῐ Ῑ Ὶ Ί Ὀ Ὁ Ὂ Ὃ

Ὄ Ὅ Ὸ Ό Ῥ Υ̓ Ῠ Ῡ Ὺ Ύ Ῥ Ὑ Ὓ Ὕ Ὗ Ω

Ὠ Ὡ Ὢ Ὣ Ὤ Ὥ Ὦ Ὧ ᾨ ᾩ ᾪ ᾫ ᾬ ᾭ ᾮ ᾯ Ω

Figure D.2   Palatino, glyphs 501–1,000. (The blank ones are spaces of various widths and types.)

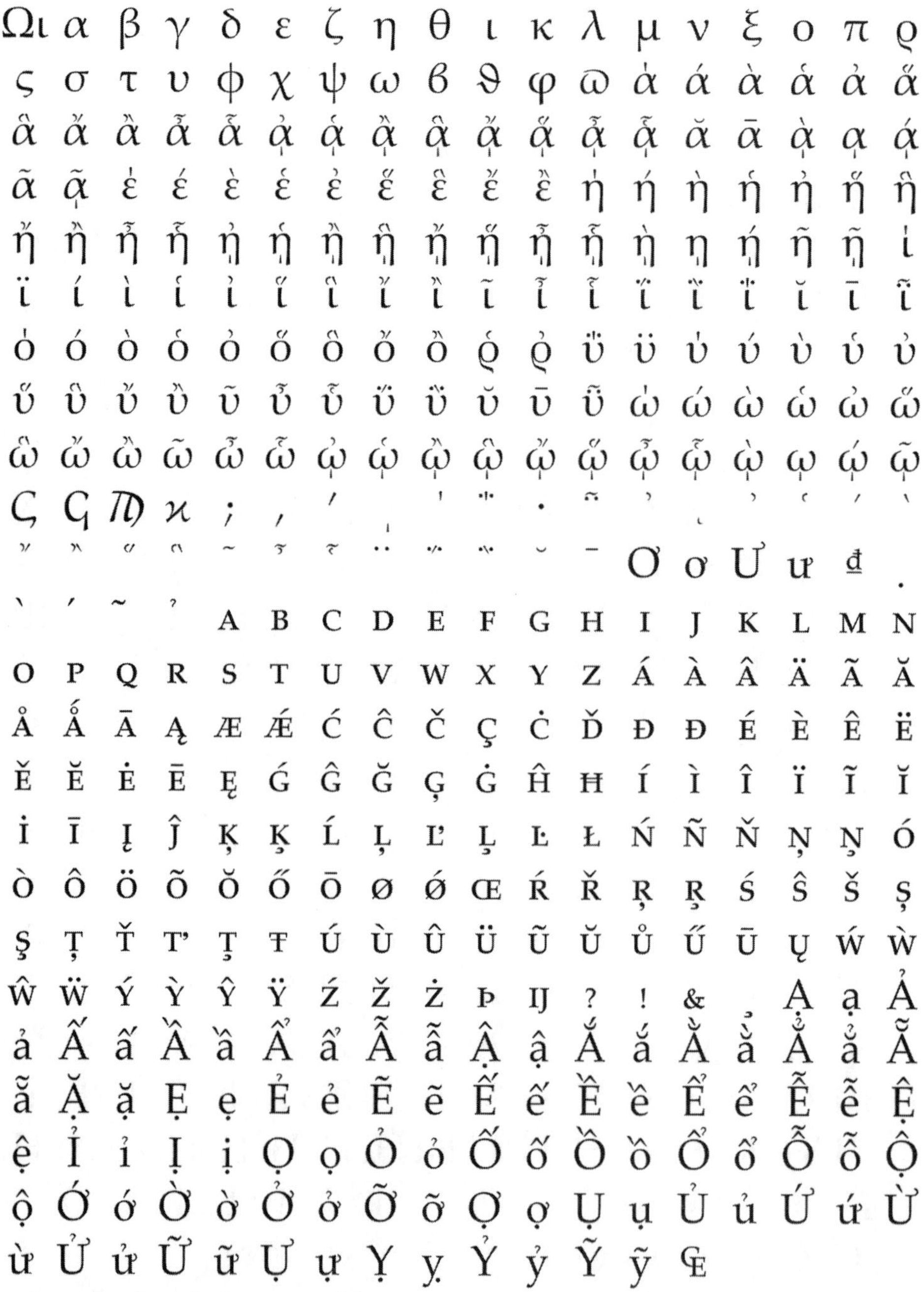

Ω ι α β γ δ ε ζ η θ ι κ λ μ ν ξ ο π ρ
ς σ τ υ φ χ ψ ω ϐ ϑ ϕ ϖ ὰ ά ᾶ ἀ ἄ ἂ
ᾶ ᾄ ᾂ ᾆ ᾀ ᾴ ᾲ ᾷ ᾳ ᾉ ᾍ ᾇ ᾁ ᾰ ᾱ ὰ ᾳ ά
ᾶ ᾷ ἐ έ ὲ ἔ ἒ ἕ ἓ ἑ ὴ ή ῆ ἠ ἤ ἢ ἥ ἣ
ἦ ἧ ῃ ᾔ ῄ ῂ ῇ ῆ ᾕ ᾓ ᾗ ᾑ ᾒ η ή ῆ ῂ ι
ϊ ί ὶ ἰ ἱ ῐ ῖ ἶ ἴ ῒ ἲ ῗ ῑ ἷ ἵ ἳ ϊ ῑ ῐ
ὀ ό ὸ ὄ ὂ ὅ ὃ ὁ ῷ ῳ ῴ ϋ ύ ὺ ύ ὺ ὕ ὓ
ὗ ὑ ὒ ῠ ῦ ὖ ὔ ῢ ῧ ΐ ῡ ῧ ὼ ώ ὠ ᾠ ὤ ὤ
ὢ ὥ ὣ ᾦ ᾤ ᾢ ῳ ῴ ῲ ῷ ῴ ᾧ ᾥ ᾣ ᾡ ῳ ῷ
Ϲ Ϲ Ⅲ ϰ ; , ΄ ʹ ῁ · ῀ ΄ ῾ ΄ ῎ ΄ ῍
῍ ῎ ῏ ῟ ῀ ῁ ῭ ·· ·· ˘ ‾   Ơ ơ Ʊ ɯ đ .
 ` ΄ ῀ ᾿   A B C D E F G H I J K L M N
O P Q R S T U V W X Y Z Á À Â Ä Ã Ă
Å Ǻ Ā Ą Æ Ǽ Ć Ĉ Č Ç Ċ Ď Đ Đ É È Ê Ë
Ě Ĕ Ė Ē Ę Ǵ Ĝ Ğ Ģ Ġ Ĥ Ħ Í Ì Î Ï Ĩ Ĭ
İ Ī Į Ĵ Ķ Ķ Ĺ Ļ Ľ Ļ Ł Ń Ñ Ň Ņ Ņ Ó
Ò Ô Ö Õ Ŏ Ő Ō Ø Ǿ Œ Ŕ Ř Ŗ Ŗ Ś Ŝ Š Ş
Ş Ţ Ť Ť' Ţ Ŧ Ú Ù Û Ü Ũ Ŭ Ů Ű Ū Ų Ẃ Ẁ
Ŵ Ẅ Ý Ỳ Ŷ Ÿ Ź Ž Ż Þ Ĳ ? ! & ₎ Ą Ą Ả
ả Ấ ấ Ầ ầ Ẩ ẩ Ẫ ẫ Ậ ậ Ắ ắ Ằ ằ Ẳ ẳ Ẵ
ẵ Ặ ặ Ẹ ẹ Ẻ ẻ Ẽ ẽ Ế ế Ề ề Ể ể Ễ ễ Ệ
ệ Ỉ ỉ Ị ị Ọ ọ Ỏ ỏ Ố ố Ồ ồ Ổ ổ Ỗ ỗ Ộ
ộ Ớ ớ Ờ ờ Ở ở Ỡ ỡ Ợ ợ Ụ ụ Ủ ủ Ứ ứ Ừ
ừ Ử ử Ữ ữ Ự ự Ỵ ỵ Ỷ ỷ Ỹ ỹ Œ

Figure D.3   Palatino, glyphs 1000–1,328

index

RELATED MANNING TITLES

The Complete Obsolete Guide to Generative AI
by David Clinton

  ISBN 9781633436985
  200 pages (estimated), $39.99
  Spring 2024 (estimated)

*Learn AI-Assisted Python Programming
with GitHub Copilot and ChatGPT*
by Leo Porter and Daniel Zingaro
Foreword by Beth Simon, Ph.D.

  ISBN 9781633437784
  296 pages, $49.99
  September 2023

Grokking Algorithms, Second Edition
by Aditya Y. Bhargava

  ISBN 9781633438538
  289 pages (estimated), $49.99
  January 2024 (estimated)

AWS for Non-Engineers
by Hiroko Nishimura

  ISBN 9781633439948
  176 pages, $39.99
  November 2022

For ordering information go to www.manning.com

The Manning Early Access Program

Don't wait to start learning! In MEAP, the Manning Early Access Program, you can read books as they're being created and long before they're available in stores.

Here's how MEAP works.

- **Start now.** Buy a MEAP and you'll get all available chapters in PDF, ePub, Kindle, and liveBook formats.

- **Regular updates.** New chapters are released as soon as they're written. We'll let you know when fresh content is available.

- **Finish faster.** MEAP customers are the first to get final versions of all books! Pre-order the print book, and it'll ship as soon as it's off the press.

- **Contribute to the process.** The feedback you share with authors makes the end product better.

- **No risk.** You get a full refund or exchange if we ever have to cancel a MEAP.

Explore dozens of titles in MEAP at www.manning.com.